Letters To Our Daughters-
Words of Wisdom For Your Journey

"Ours is not the task of fixing the entire world at once, but of stretching out to mend the part of the world that is within our reach."

— Clarissa Pinkola Estés

Table of Contents

Introduction - Alaina Reichwald 5

Blessed, Sacred Daughters Of The New World 7

Fear Not... (Or Fear And Do It Anyway) 9

Peaks And Valleys 15

Change By Choice 19

Believing In Yourself 22

There Is Only One You! 28

Trust In Yourself 32

Find Your Voice 34

Be Your Own Guru 38

Give It All You Got 44

It's What's On The Inside That Count 47

Be A Rainbow 51

Do As I Say, Not As I Do 56

Supernova 58

The Universe Begins With You 67

On Honesty, Respect And Manners 69

College Bound 72

Manifest Within 76

Let Intuition Lead *87*

Your Inner Spark *90*

Open Hearted Vulnerability *95*

Rules Are Made To Be Broken *99*

Don't Worry, You Can Figure It Out *104*

Be Courageous Enough To Be You *111*

The Road Less Traveled *113*

The Power Of A Smile *116*

Gossip Girl *124*

Safe Harbor *127*

In Deepest Gratitude And Honor: *131*

Introduction - Alaina Reichwald

To Our Collective Daughters,

At this time in history, many of us are feeling the need to embrace all our young women, and pass down a lineage of self love; gratitude; compassion and the ability to engage our world from a place of power. We want you to know that each of you are held in the embrace of groups of collective mommies. We care for each one of you and wish for you a wonderful adventure as you grow up and create your own unique life journey.

This collection of letters was inspired one day in December 2013. I stood in my bathroom blow drying my hair. My daughter and I had just had a contentious conversation and there was so much I wanted to say to her. But during this particular time, she didn't feel like listening to any lengthy conversation, or words of advice. I knew this was normal for her age, but there was so much I wanted to share with her about friendships, school, understanding herself. Thinking about this, I realized that maybe I could write all my thoughts down in letters and then share them with her for one day when she might be open and interested. That thought led to another thought. I have so many wise and thoughtful women in my life, and I imagined they had passions and interests that were not at the forefront of my mind. They could contribute so much of their own perspective and wisdom as a gift to not only my daughter but to the collective young woman energy. The idea for a book was formed.

What you will be reading here is a truly remarkable array of wise words. Although it was created with our young women in mind, I have gained so much insight and inspiration reading these words myself. They are timeless and ageless. I'm so grateful for the mommies that came along with me on this journey.

Collectively, we hope the words on these pages will allow you to think about things that may have not yet emerged in your awareness or give you guidance when you feel stuck. More then anything, we hope these words empower you to become all you are meant to be. Remember, there are no accidents. You are here for a purpose. You are one of a kind. There is nobody else like you on this entire planet! You don't need to figure anything out or be anything... except YOURSELF!

Alaina Reichwald, May 2016

Blessed, sacred daughters of the New World:

I honor you and make way for empowered humans to walk the Earth. You are whole and complete for this task as your birthright. I seek only to correct for the negativity of our collective past.

Somewhere along the way of recent human history, we lost connection with All-That-Is by our own choices. It is our birthright to be connected to everything. It is our birthright to be whole and joyful and empowered to create for ourselves that which feeds our joyful passion. We are doing it now, every day. When I wake in the morning, I consciously design my day. I consciously attract that which feeds my empowerment and joy.

What is empowerment? It is that which frees me to step out of myself and do what I know is right. How do I know what is right? It is that which calls to me most powerfully; that which brings joy into my heart, so that I do it smiling and dancing; that which calls me to want to connect with All-That-Is in joy. I give myself permission to do THAT thing in every moment. When I do THAT thing, I am a gift to everyone and everything around me. That is my sovereign path.

I don't have to be perfect, and I can evolve myself through experience. I am more empowered and more joyful with every step on my path. As a sovereign, I take responsibility for what I create and I can change it whenever I choose. To change my experience, I change my thoughts. That is why I go to sleep in gratitude and I wake with conscious thoughts of what I wish to create. I have a new opportunity every day, so it gets better and better. This is the science of personal responsibility and it is more true for me than listening to the authority of anyone else. If I feel pain or happiness, I know I created it and I know how to change it. Only I can know what is my path on this Earth. Nobody else can make decisions for me.

When I conduct my life in this way, I am an authentic leader for everyone around me. I am consciously connected to everything, so I know exactly how to do my part. Humans are re-learning conscious connectivity and they look for examples in those around them that hold strong inner authority.

So breathe in the power of the Universe, and breathe out fear. YOU are in control of your life. Have fun!

Love,
Alluvia
Alluvia Love, February 2014

FEAR NOT... (or fear and do it anyway)

"What is needed, rather than running away or controlling or suppressing or any other resistance, is understanding fear; that means, watch it, learn about it, come directly into contact with it. We are to learn about fear, not how to escape from it."

— Jiddu Krishnamurti

Dear Daughter,

Since you were old enough to voice your opinion, I have witnessed and admired your fearless knowing of yourself. When you were younger, you had this stubborn knowing about what you were and were not willing to do. Although having such a strong sense of who you are can have challenges, it is something many adults search for their whole lives. It was also a time when you appeared fearless. Your expression was determined when faced with new challenges.

Now, when I see the areas where you struggle, I want to step in and offer you stories of how I struggled in the same areas... I want to help you navigate this unfamiliar terrain, but where a few years ago, you sought out and welcomed my wisdom, you now understandably want to figure much of it out on your own.

Fear is one of the greatest challenges and lessons on our life's journey. One of my favorite quotes, and one that hangs in my office, is by Neal Donald Walsh- "Life begins at the end of your comfort zone". And it is at the end of the comfort zone that many of us experience the sensation of Fear.

Fear of the new; fear of the unknown; fear of the unexpected; and even just the fear of the unknowable.

And it is also the place where life, excitement and adventure begins.

Fear is one of the most basic and powerful human energies, and it has been and continues to be used to control people. People are easily controlled when they are afraid... the illusion that backing away from the fear = safety. This is not always true.

At its core, fear is meant to heighten our instincts and help us to survive a saber tooth tiger in our village. Or any impending, life threatening danger. When we are standing on top of a high precipice about to jump off on the longest zip-line ever, we may feel a tension building in our bodies. Our hearts may be pounding loudly in our chests and our hands may be shaking a little. We may be sweating and feel uncomfortable... like we want to run. This is that overt physical fear.

We know it and expect it and often if we want to do something badly enough we choose to overcome it. But the covert fear is something quite different and much less tangible. It is the fear that prevents us from taking risks. It may show up as fear of failure; or fear of the unknown; or fear of owning ourselves completely. Sometimes we fear doing things on our own, or it may be a fear of doing things differently than our friends, or our family agrees with.

Of course, there are some things as your mom that I want you to be afraid of because they can hurt you. I want you to have a healthy fear of serious drugs because they have the ability to alter the plans for a healthy and successful life. I want you to be afraid of dark alleys in dangerous neighborhoods and avoid going down them. I want you to be afraid of getting into a car of a stranger who offers you a ride.

Then there are times when I want you to be able to recognize that what you are feeling is fear. I want you to be able to navigate the corners of these feelings and move through them towards what you desire.

When you feel fear about trying out for a part in a play, I want you to face that fear and keep moving forward. When you have big feelings for another person and are trying to decide if you should give the relationship a try, I want you to go for it enjoying the adventure of getting to know someone on a deeper level. If a friend introduces you to a challenging adventure, I want you to grab that opportunity and go for it. These experiences are what make life zing with excitement.

Life is short ... and so many of us get stuck in the routine of life. We rarely move out of our comfort zone and into the discomfort of the unfamiliar. Yet, often it is in the space of that discomfort that amazing, life altering adventures happen. Many of my most wonderful, life altering adventures happened when I pushed (or was pushed) through my own fear. Going to sleep away camp, traveling to distant places, going to college, moving away from my family, getting married, having YOU! (honestly just to name a few). Each of these adventures produced great fear, and yet, my life would be much less rich and full without having walked through these these feelings and reaping the rewards that came with them.

Here are some ways I have found to help me work with and, when necessary, push through my fear:

1. Recognize the sensation of fear. Know all the ways fear shows itself to you. This may change over time, but the better you get to know it, the less crafty and manipulative it can become. There comes a time when you see the fear creeping in and you can invite it to join you for tea. You can sit with it, talk to it, understand it... and through the process be present with it. Then, it holds much less power. Never run from fear... it loves a good chase.

2. Learn to use your breath. Our slow deep breath has the power to shift our physical state. Learn to use this tool to help you get back to yourself when you are feeling afraid.

3. Sometimes our bodies need to move in order to process the adrenaline that it releases during fearful times. Once we move that energy out of our system, we can often think more clearly and calmly. Just going for a run around the block can transform the fear.

4. Feel the fear and do it anyway. Be present with it and allow it to show all its parts to you. Don't let fear control decisions that you know will be in your best interest. Don't let fear turn you around from a great new possibility.

5. Engage in some form of meditation. This allows you to come back to and know yourself deeply. It allows you to sit in the presence of discomfort , painful, and challenging thoughts, and create great self knowledge. Even if you just sit with a

question for a few minutes a day, you will develop your inner guidance and intuition and the ability to know deep down what is best for you. This will stop the fear stories from taking root.

There is nothing that will completely remove fear from your life. Having a deep understanding of how it shows up for you and how to navigate through it has the power to change your life completely. It is my deepest and greatest hope that you grow the ability to work with your personal landscape of fear and overcome any obstacles that block your path to the greatest success and happiness imaginable.

Love, Mom

Alaina Reichwald, December 2013

PEAKS AND VALLEYS

"When you get into a tight place and everything goes against you, till it seems that you can not hold on for a minute longer, never give up then, for that is just the place and time that the tide will turn".

— Harriet Beecher Stowe

Dear Daughter,

The past few years of my life have been filled with many highs and lows. It seems as the older I get the more meaning I can extract from life's peaks & valleys. Also in the past few years there have been a few people in our community who have taken their own lives. Each time we hear the news of this happening, we see how it affects everyone close to that individual. The pain it causes the families and friends. The news becomes the focus of our dinnertime conversations. I appreciate your ability and willingness to discuss difficult subjects openly with your family and voice your opinion so clearly. You had said that nothing can be so bad to take your own life and that it is a selfish act. That really struck a chord in me. Hearing you say that made me want to pull you into my arms to tell you how right you were...Peaks & Valleys.

We are surrounded in life by all sorts of cycles: sunrise, sunset, season's change, earth rotates, shooting stars fall from the sky. We all experience cycles too, times when everything is moving along effortlessly, our days are connecting together smoothly and we are feeling good about ourselves. We feel loved deeply by those around us and put out love and positive energy everywhere we go. During these "peak" cycles we have more energy, more patience, more compassion, and more love for others and ourselves. Happiness can be seen and it is contagious: we are drawn to people who are happy and friendly. If I am having a rough day and I cross paths with someone who exhibits kindness towards me I usually feel better. Also, when I am having a rough day and come across someone having a rougher day, if I extend kindness to them, often it makes me and the other person feel better.

There are also cycles where you can't seem to do anything right, nothing falls into place, everything you do requires tremendous effort, or you don't feel like you are being heard. These "valley" cycles can make you feel alone, isolated and unloved. We all want to feel a sense of belonging, inclusion, love, and happiness. During these cycles when it seems to require all your strength to keep moving forward is when we experience tremendous growth. The same way that happiness can draw people towards us, sadness can keep people away. When someone acts out in a mean or spiteful way towards others, it often means they feel sad or lonely or misunderstood. Being kind towards others is much easier when we are feeling good about ourselves.

Another way to look at Peaks & Valleys is that they co-exist; you can't have one without the other. In order to enjoy the view from the mountains peak you must first walk through the valleys. When I'm feeling low and lacking the energy to do anything about it sometimes all it takes is a happy thought, beautiful sight, or kind words to cause a shift inside me. Other times it just takes a hug from the right person and I start to feel my tank filling back up with love, confidence and happiness. What I realize during these shifts is that love, confidence and happiness always live within me and I just need the proper fuel to get them active again. Some of the things I would want you to remember during one of those more difficult moments is: 1. Get outside into nature if at all possible. Somehow being in the presence of trees, dirt, mountains, desert, wildlife tends to reset our sense of inner well-being. Even if you don't feel like it... GO. 2. Call a friend or a family member who is a good listener. Tell them that you are going through a Valley and need some support. If people know you need them, they can be there for you. Often our tendency is to withdraw from all those who care about us, which can make us feel lonely and isolated. So REACH OUT. 3. Remember, pain often accompanies Valley's. The pain is normal and will pass if you let it come up and honor it completely. Don't be afraid to allow all your feelings and express your sadness or frustration.

Some lows in life are inevitable and unavoidable. When my dad passed away, suddenly and unexpectedly, I was devastated. I missed him so deeply I was not sure how to move forward without him in my life. What I later realized after his death was the reason I was so sad is that he brought so much joy to my life. I have many wonderful memories of my father and he still brings me joy. I feel his love and influence even though he left this life.

You are strong, resilient, and capable. When you travel through the peaks & valleys of life I want you to remember these things about yourself. When you're feeling good standing tall on a mountain top, help others get up to you. When you're trudging through the valleys and you feel all alone, it's OK to ask for help.

With much love,

Mom

Annie Seelenfreund, 2013

CHANGE BY CHOICE

"The greatest discovery of all time is that a person can change her future just by changing her attitude".

— Oprah Winfrey

Dear Daughter,

You say you can't change how you are. Trust me in your lifetime you will change so much. You have massive abilities to change when it is something you want to do. You can say "I don't want to change. OR I'm not going to change", but you absolutely can change. You will be in relationships in your life where the only way to improve or continue them is to make some changes.

I understand that you are easily irritated and that may last for awhile. Feeling irritated and acting irritated are two completely different things. You can feel irritated and then make choices about how you are going to handle that irritation for the best results. If you get into a habit of showing your irritation every time you feel it, that will be reflected to you in all sorts of ways by the people around you. And rarely is it a positive reflection.

The sooner you begin to separate your irritated feelings from your actions, the sooner you will find more peaceful interactions with the people in your life. Words and tone are different things... and tone is MUCH more powerful then any words you are saying.

Here's the deal... and there is really no pussy footing around all this... that we can get all irritated with people around us... they bug us and trigger us... and we often forget the bigger picture. Which is that life is transient... nobody is promised a tomorrow. We all live life constantly forgetting this.

And I think it's important to remember that... not to be fearful, but rather to engage the quality of gratitude. To treat each other kindly, respectfully, knowing that there may not be a tomorrow. We naturally operate on default where we assume there will always be a tomorrow. But as you have seen in your very young life, that is not the case. And as sad as I am for you to have experienced the death of a dear friend at such a young age, you have also received a gift if you are willing to accept it... the gift of really knowing that any time, unexpectedly, life can dramatically change. This happens all around us, and if we wake up and pay attention, those awarenesses can help us see the things that are important.

I'm not saying even for a second that you can stop from feeling irritated...or even that you should feel bad about being irritated. Sometimes I feel very irritated by people around me... sometimes I know the reason, and other times I have no idea why... but I try to choose not to hurt them with my unexplained irritation.

Sometimes it can help to wake up and set the intention that you are going to practice being loving and generous with your kindness. I think you love being the recipient of kindness and gratitude... and if so, put as much out there as you can... and before you know it you will have created a new habit that returns to you even bigger then what you put out there. Ask in each situation how you can brighten someone's day or make them feel appreciated or loved.

Mom

Alaina Reichwald, 2013

BELIEVING IN YOURSELF

"Love yourself. Forgive yourself. Be true to yourself. How you treat yourself sets the standard for how others will treat you."

— Steve Maraboli

"Keep your dreams alive. Understand to achieve anything requires faith and belief in yourself, vision, hard work, determination, and dedication. Remember all things are possible for those who believe."

-Gail Devers, Olympic athlete, retired three-time Olympic champion in track and field for the US Olympic Team.

My Beautiful Daughters,

Believing in and loving who you are is one of the greatest gifts you can give to yourself.

When you were little, it was natural for you to feel joy all the time. The smallest things brought you great happiness. You did not compare yourself to others. You accepted others as they were and you accepted yourself as you were. Life was full of peace, love and joy.

As the years go by and you reach adolescence, the first experiences of self- judgment, self-doubt, comparing yourself to others and feeling like you do not fit in may start to affect you. You may start to question that confident feeling that all is okay. Outside influences, such as the perception of being judged by others, gossiping, bullying, changing friends, can also affect how you feel.

Allowing yourself to let in thoughts that make you feel insecure, down, sad, angry, and fearful can crush your self esteem. These negative thoughts and feelings are part of being human and need understanding and care. Instead of fighting it, paying attention to how you react to things, understanding the source of your insecurities, and taking steps to address your concerns. Realizing that you are in control of the thoughts which lead to the feelings about yourself can be freeing.

The way we talk to ourselves is so important. If you find yourself saying, "I can't", "I don't know", or "What if"?, you can try to change your "I can't" to "I can't do it yet, but I am working on it." If you ask, " What if I fail?", you can replace it with "Then I will try again." How we talk to ourselves is very powerful and has a profound impact on how we interact with the world around us, especially other people.

Practice being your own best friend. You deserve to treat yourself well. After all, you have the rest of your life to spend with yourself. Treat yourself as you do someone you love and admire. You are capable and worthy. You are stronger than you believe.

You can look at your life as a team. You are in charge of who is going to be on your side. Some choices are inspiration, truth, gratitude, enthusiasm, ambition, worry, anger, fear, blame and sadness. Choose the positive teammates and you will always win the game. One of the ways you can show that you love and trust yourself is taking a close look at who is on your "team".

How we love and accept ourselves directly affects the quality of our relationships with others, our work, our free time, our faith and our future. Loving ourselves is an on-going daily process, not a one time event. It begins by wrapping yourself up in your own affection and appreciation.

Believing in yourself is a vital survival skill. You will enhance the quality of your life by feeling worthwhile, and by believing that you can affect circumstances and situations in your life.

When needing inspiration to care for yourself, reaching into your own "personal toolbox" to help you get back on track. Here are a few of my favorites:

-'Loving What Is' by Byron Katie

The author of this book presents "The Work" which is essentially four questions to help us work through personal struggles, especially in our thought process. Think of the situation or thought and ask yourself the following questions:

-"Is it true?"

-"Can I absolutely know that it's true?" -"How do I react when I think that thought?"

-"Who would I be without that thought?" When I ask these questions, I am always amazed at how much easier it is to gain a new perspective and I often feel like a weight has been lifted off of my shoulders.

-The Four Agreements' by Don Miguel Ruiz The author of this book has helped me get back on track with my thoughts, words and actions when relating to others.

The Four Agreements are:

1. Be Impeccable with your Word and Speak with integrity. Say only what you mean. Avoid using the Word to speak against yourself or to gossip about others. Use the power of your Word in the direction of truth and love. Growing up, we often learn that it is normal to talk unkindly about others. We don't realize how powerful our spoken

word is and how much it impacts our relationships and interactions with those around us, including ourselves.

2. Don't Take Anything Personally

"Nothing others do is because of you. What others say and do is a projection of their own reality. When you are immune to the opinions and actions of others, you won't be the victim of needless suffering". As a teenager, this is really hard to do. Often we feel that everything is about us, especially how we perceive other's are treating us.

3. Don't Make Assumptions

"Find the courage to ask questions and to express what you really want. Communicate with others as clearly as you can to avoid misunderstandings, sadness and drama. With just this one agreement, you can completely transform your life." Sometimes, I have found that taking things personally and making assumptions can go hand in hand. And this Agreement goes hand in hand with The Work, by Byron Katie. Ask questions to determine if what you think is actually true in any setting. When we ask questions to clarify our thoughts and feelings, we are often pleasantly surprised that our worry was unfounded.

4. Always Do Your Best

"Your best is going to change from moment to moment; it will be different when you are healthy as opposed to sick. Under any circumstance, simply do your best, and you will avoid self-judgment, self-abuse, and regret."

Mommy

Cindy Burson, December 2013

THERE IS ONLY ONE YOU!

(How's That For Important)

"If you celebrate your differentness, the world will, too. It believes exactly what you tell it—through the words you use to describe yourself, the actions you take to care for yourself, and the choices you make to express yourself. Tell the world you are one-of-a-kind creation who came here to experience wonder and spread joy. Expect to be accommodated."

— Victoria Moran

Dear Daughter,

Think about it! There is only one you in this entire world. If you really think about that for awhile, it can almost bend your mind. Often, we forget how unbelievably unique we are. We spend so much time comparing ourselves to others or even sometimes trying to be like someone else. But once we begin to practice really liking and even loving our own uniqueness, other's tend to love us more also.

Here are some tips for loving, trusting and caring for yourself:

1. Give yourself a positive first thought when you wake up, and a loving last thought before bed. Believe with all your heart that you have and deserve joy, happiness, love, health and peace. At first this might take effort, but it's an

28

experiment with nothing to lose. See what happens when you begin offering loving, kind, and caring thoughts to yourself. You will most likely begin to believe those things. Our mind always believes the things it tells itself the most often.

2. **Take time to journal.** By writing down thoughts and events in your day, can help you keep a record of memories and help you work through events in your life. If something is challenging during the day, you can write it down at night before bed and even ask your inner self to come up with some solutions while you sleep. Your unconscious mind is powerful and also a wonderful problem solver. Sometimes it just needs some quiet time to come up with good solutions.

3. **Talk yourself happy** by helping your mind to become more positive and feel lighter. Try listening to happy, uplifting music, and think about what you are grateful for. Gratitude for even the smallest things in your life have a way of resetting your mind and refocusing you towards appreciation instead of feeling like things are never right or enough.

4. **Expand your interests** by learning and experiencing something new and fun by yourself, with friends or with family. When we are so busy with school, homework, friends, chores it can be difficult to consider trying something new. BUT when we step out of our comfort zone and reach into a

new place we often feel more excited and enthusiastic about our lives. We begin to see endless possibilities, instead of boring routine of what we do every day.

*5. **Exercise** by hiking, biking, swimming, skiing, doing yoga or other activities that inspire you. Take care of your body and your body will take care of you.*

*6. **Eat well** by putting organic and seasonal food into your body. This practice will keep you healthy, help you to feel good and energized. Food is fuel for your body in the same way that gas is fuel for your car. You will get better mileage and feel better with certain foods over others. Get to know what your body likes by paying attention to how it feels after you eat.*

*7. **Be patient with yourself.** Life is about learning and growing... most of us don't get things right immediately.*

*8. **Live in gratitude**- you cannot be in gratitude and have negative thoughts and feelings at the same time. Focus on what you are blessed with, and focus on what you have gratitude for no matter how large or small.*

*9. **Listen to your intuition** by looking for signs and pay attention to your gut feelings. You have a whole inner world that knows so much about all the situations you find yourself in if you slow down enough to listen. Ask yourself a question* and then sit quietly so your intuition has time and space to communicate with you. You will be amazing at the amount of creativity you will find.

*10. **Forgive yourself** and others by giving yourself permission to move on with your life and let go of any negative thoughts that hold you back and produce stress. 11. Sleep well.*

*12. **Affirmations** help us to stay in positive, happy, uplifting thoughts and energize us toward a happy day! Choose or create affirmations that work for you in your life and repeat them daily.*

13. List your successes

Keep a file of cards, awards, pictures, feedback, articles, journal entries, mementos that remind you of how awesome you are. These lists can offer much support and positive feedback when we are feeling low.

Think about creating your own Personal Life Toolbox. What did you read here that you might consider putting in yours?

Love, Mom

Cindy Burson, December 2013

TRUST IN YOURSELF

"People always ask me, 'What is it that you regret?' And I say, 'nothing, because I could not buy what I've learned'. And I apply those things to my life. And hopefully, hopefully, it helps me be a better human in the future and make better choices."

— Katy Perry

Dear Daughter,

Go easy on yourself and learn to trust in YOU. Trust in your choices and your abilities. Trust that you will make mistakes and learn from them. Often when we are on the cusp between childhood and adulthood, we are filled with internal conflict. You are figuring out who you are as an individual, separate from your family. You will find yourself making choices that are different from them, and you will sometimes wonder if you are wrong. Sometimes you will be. But as long as you are listening to yourself and trusting your own judgment, and no one else's, you will always land on your feet.

Although your judgement is the final filter, don't hesitate to seek advice, ask good questions, think critically about the advice you receive, and consider the unique perspective of the advice-giver. Then make your own choice, one that rings true to your heart. You make choices every day, from the mundane to the monumental. What to eat for breakfast, which friends to hold dear. As you grow, your choices will become of greater consequence. Will you continue to challenge yourself academically? Where will you go to college? What will you decide to study? Where will you live? How do you picture your life when you are my age? Who will you choose to share your life with? How will you make a difference in this world? As you face these daunting questions, I want you to know that you are not expected to know the answers right away. I had no idea when I was your age that I would end up living where we live, doing what I do, and how I would be giving back to my community. But I did follow my heart in every decision I made, which led me straight to this wonderful fulfilling life surrounded by people I love and admire.

Follow your own path and you will never find a shortage of people who want to walk by your side. Even then, know that it is YOUR choice who you allow to walk by your side. Surround yourself by people who challenge you to be your best, authentic self. People who love you for the person you are and the choices you make.

DFTBA,

Mom

Cristina Wooley, Jan 2014

FIND YOUR VOICE

"I speak not for myself but for those without a voice...those that have fought for their rights... their right to live in peace, their right to be treated with dignity, their right to equality of opportunity, their right to be educated."

— Malala Yousafzai

Dear Daughters,

I am writing this letter to you to express what is, in my opinion, a very important part of life's journey. I am a bit biased because it has been a particularly vital part of my path. Find Your Voice.

The concept of "my voice" has centered around my own unique way of viewing the world, and my ability to express that. I believe we all have a distinct filter through which we view the world. Sometimes this can make our individual experiences a bit lonely, as we begin to realize that not everyone sees through our filter. What we are rarely taught is: that's ok! That's what makes this experience of being human so exciting and adventurous. We are not a bunch of zombies and robots, we are unique individuals with a special story to tell, and so many different choices as to how we choose to tell it.

From my experience, I see that everyone has a way of

expressing themselves so differently. Their perspectives; what they find important; what they want to share. Even mothers can be challenged in understanding the way their children see and express that Voice. Sometimes our daughters even teach us how to use our Voice by the power in which they express themselves in the world. I knew that even when I didn't understand your way of doing or seeing things, I had to honor your "filter", your unique "lens" through which you experienced the world around you.

There has been no greater joy and honor than bearing witness to your gifts blossoming and developing. For me, that is what "your voice" is all about. It is seeing the seedling of it when you are born, watering it, nurturing it, helping you to love it, and then sitting back and watching it take off.

Sometimes, as your voice begins to come forward, it can at times feel intimidating. The power of what it holds can at times feel like a volcano, ready to bubble up and erupt. Your voice gives you the power and courage to say what is in your heart and on your mind. Your voice truly allows you to see others even at times when it feels like what you have to say collides with someone else. Your voice brings strength and conviction concerning who you are and what you believe and feel. Never let anyone take that from you, and most importantly, never give it away.

My advice to you is to let your heart and your mind work together in navigating through your life. I say this because that is the advice I've been giving myself for many years. The two together are unstoppable, truly.

Never be afraid to express your feelings, even if they come out a bit on the passionate side. While the world might occasionally tell you to "pipe down", let that be the queue to shout it from the mountaintops. Having a strong voice can often make others uncomfortable, but that does not mean you have to be quiet. Honing your skills in communicating compassionately, bringing together your intellect and your heart, these are the keys to having your voice be heard.

We have lived in a world for many thousands of years that encourages action, force and doing things with a loud voice. Sometimes your voice can be expressed quietly or through a heartfelt connection to those around you, and your ability to soften in the presence of aggravation and chaos. Creativity connects us to the mysteries of life. It will bring you great pleasure throughout your life.

As women, it is often perceived that our voices are "weaker" than mens'. I do not hold this belief, and I encourage you not to as well. Our feminine voice is just different from a man's. Many women, understandably, have decided to follow the premise of "if you can't beat em', join 'em". Instead of honoring their own unique feminine voice, they have joined the ranks and taken on a more masculine voice. There is absolutely nothing wrong with this, and in some ways it has helped the feminine voice be heard, but I would encourage you to find your own feminine voice as well. There is something beautiful, mysterious, yes, and a bit dangerous about the feminine voice. Don't shy away from this. It is part of your strength and your wisdom as women, and again, you will bring it forward in the world with your own unique signature.

In closing, what I would say is if what I say does not resonate in you, if you don't feel it deeply, then put it aside. You and only you are the determiner of who you are and what you want to say. You are at the helm, and always will be. And your unique gift, voice, whatever you want to call it, will continue to grow and evolve. These words are just meant to offer a gentle guidance to who you already are. But ultimately YOU are the one to define that.

Love ALWAYS Mommy

Darsie White, December 2013

BE YOUR OWN GURU

"Go forth and journey with God and your soul first and foremost, for to be Divinely Selfish is a great gift of Love. To betray yourself at the risk of betraying another is the biggest betrayal of all. Thank you God for this strength, I know it is You because I, of myself, cannot do this alone.... Please help me.... I surrender.... In humility..."

My Darling Daughter,

I imagine one day, you too will be writing and contemplating your life, what you received from your family, parents and friends. What gifts they all gave to you, some of which feel "positive", and some which feel "negative".

I am grateful to my parents and family, for they have shown me love, and what is not love. They taught me how to work hard, how to go and push beyond my perceived limitations, how to think and solve problems for myself. They taught me how to pretend, to put a smile on my face and make (believe) others think everything is perfect. They taught me shame, judgment, guilt, persecution and how to hide within my tiny self. They taught me how to wait until the grass is greener before I live my life, how to be jealous and compare and value my life by measuring it off of other people. They taught me how to live in poverty and abundance. They taught me how to give freely, and how to give with strings attached.

They taught me fear, lack, insecurity, loneliness, isolation, repression and how to self criticize. I was taught self-reliance, arrogance, pride and apathy.

My family also taught me how to use my mind, to solve puzzles, to see and create solutions. They taught me independence, self discovery, silence, quiet support. They taught me the benefits and consequences of self choice.

What you resist persists darling, there is no way around unless the truth is denied. Only through the barriers does freedom come. Have the courage to walk through the fierce fire of purification, and you will be graced with all the support you need along the way!

When a person gets sick in certain tribes in Africa, the community comes together because that person is the voice of the collective. There is something out of alignment with the whole tribe. The tribe gathers round and listens to this person until he/she feels heard. The illness is shared amongst the collective and the burden to bear is not one alone's to carry. When it is your turn, step up and have the courage to be the voice of truth. When it is someone else's turn to speak out, hold the space to listen to their voice, and bring such tremendous humility and resolve, and action to realign yourself and the whole community into harmony.

So, what can I say?

~ Be your own guru. Be aware of those who want you to follow them and be your guide, instead of empowering you to be confident in following your own intuition. You might piss other people off to follow your own path and not what they think is right for you. Humbly listen as others have much to offer and show up in your life for a reason, but also learn how to be discerning so you don't believe and blindly follow what does not matter for you. Trust and follow your own guidance anyway, the truth is worth it!

~ Take time to give and receive. It is said that if you ever need a helping hand, you'll find one at the end of your arm. And a time always comes when you discover that you have two hands, one for helping yourself, one for helping others. Do your best to offer your gifts with Unconditional Love, without expectation of any return or reciprocation. The world does not "Owe" you anything. Reciprocation does not always come from the same two people in fair exchange, but quite often shows up in very unexpected ways in life, be grateful when it shows up for you, and instead of having jealousy or being in competition, practice gratitude when it shows up for others, happy for them that they are receiving in life as well! If the jealousy does show up, be with it and own it within yourself until it dissolves back into the softness and grace of love.

~ Have the courage to take action and push yourself beyond what you thought was possible, way past the point of what you thought yourself to be capable of. I bet you'll surprise yourself! If you choose, do God's Will. Find God in everything. Explore where God is and where God is not. For example, every religion on Earth has God. And every religion also has ideals that is "not God". Some things are just made up by man for one reason or another and is masked as God, but it is merely the will of man, invested in a certain outcome. It's up to you to discern what works and what doesn't.

~ Take responsibility for absolutely everything in your life. When you have the humility to do this for yourself, it teaches others that it is okay for them to step up in a safe place without feeling judged or condemned as well, and you'll notice them making choices to take responsibility for their own lives also. Everything is of our own creations! We are powerful manifestors, creating all the joy and sorrow in an effort to experience life completely. Everything is the Law of the Mirror, whatever you see in others is all here to show you who you are. What a GIFT this PRESENCE is! Be impeccable, present, in integrity, authentic, real.

~ Be flexible, be stupid! Change is constant, make

mistakes on purpose. Grow up, but also stay a child. Be humble, admit your mistakes, apologize and easily forgive. Sometimes you just have to laugh at life and all the curve balls, sometimes you cry about them. The important thing though is not to stay stuck in it. Get good at recognizing what it feels like when you're stuck, then make the choice to feel it, or move in a different direction. Life is in constant motion, even if it's the movement of stillness. I don't know who said it, but I heard when life ends up flowing in an unexpected and strange way, just stand up like the heroine of a novel and yell "PLOT TWIST", and move forward with gusto into this new journey!

~ Be grateful for God in your life, for your ancestors who walked this path before you, for your true friends, for truth, for life, and hold sacred reverence for all of life in immaculate, meticulous, deep and pure gratitude out of the sheer joy of being alive! Help yourself to healthy servings of Divine Selfishness so that you may always live your life authentically, being the grace and change in the world. Pursue your passions and what brings you joy, dance, theatre, art, singing, bodywork, writing, teaching, or whatever else it is, bring all of you into your passion and boldly create what you want. The only one who will ever stop you is yourself.

I love you so very much, but, you already know that! Love yourself and God first, and you'll never question love from anyone. I see you for who you really are, and I am so grateful you continually bless life in every way. Thank you for being you!

Love,

A grateful woman who is honored to call herself your Mom

Gaial Bowen, 2015

GIVE IT ALL YOU GOT

"Perseverance is not a long race; it is many short races one after the other."

— Walter Elliot

Dear Daughter,

There will be times that things are hard and you want to give up.

You may think that you are not good enough to accomplish what you are attempting.

Please, remember, don't give up.

In the book Outliers, Malcolm Gladwell, says it takes approximately 10,000 hours of practice to gain mastery in any field.

And in our culture, there seems to be this belief that we need to be good at something right away or we will just stop doing it.

But remember, it took time to learn to walk and run. You fell down many many times. It took time (and a number of crashes) to be able to ride your bike. Swimming. Learning to read was a slow, methodical process that now you can do beautifully.

Things worth learning can take time to master. But you absolutely can master it as long as you commit to the art of moving forward. Slow and Steady wins the race. I know that was the case for me. I always loved Spanish, but when not becoming fluent quickly, I gave up often only to take the language up again and again throughout the years. I love going to Spanish speaking countries and I want more then anything to learn the language.

After many false starts, I decided not to have expectations or impatience, but rather to keep plugging away. Even if it takes me ten years, I know now I can get there. With consistent practice, I can possibly even get there more quickly.

It has been a year, and during my last visit to Mexico, I could speak more than I ever have before. Am I fluent? So far from it. But each little moment of progress tells me that I am on the path towards one of my many dreams. Not working towards something interesting to you only means you're not getting any closer. You'll be stuck in that same place 1, 3, 5 years from now instead of being completely capable (or fluent) by that time.

Don't let any of your desires or dreams seem out of reach. Just tell yourself with patience and determination you can achieve absolutely anything.

And when we do this, growth and learning is FUN!

Love,

Mom

Alaina Reichwald, 2014

IT'S WHAT'S ON THE INSIDE THAT COUNT

"Outer beauty attracts, but inner beauty captivates."

— Kate Angell

My Dear Girl,

Any critical ideas you have about your body and physical appearance do not belong to you. The way you criticize your body, and examine and judge, each area with distaste did not crop up from your inner spirit.

This is a cultural demon that women and men struggle with every single day of their lives by the images that they see repeatedly through all sorts of media.

I have fought these demons everyday for as long as I remember. When my body has been all different sizes. This cultural poison will grow and waste so much precious time if you let it take over.

You are bombarded by these false images in all the television shows you immerse yourself in. You fall in love with these characters, but what you don't realize is they teach you to hate your body, your face, your personality. They try to make you believe that what you see on the screen is perfection. Behind the scene, you don't see the make up, wardrobe, writers, editors, and for many of them, their own self destructive thoughts about themselves.. Or their mental stress of not being someone else's idea of perfect. At your tender age of adolescence, if you let your guard down, and don't question your beliefs about your body, you will find yourself a slave to these thoughts and criticisms. They will take up so much of your power and energy that could be used for good. They will infiltrate your relationships. They will force you to compare yourself to others, and create judgement and hate where it doesn't need to exist. Your self love as well as your love of others will fall prey to this mindset.

When our minds are absorbed daily in examining, questioning and criticizing our physical appearance, that energy leaves little time for the creation of love. Of giving, of really being there for others. Vanity is a sad, but prevalent state of affairs in our culture. And the media reinforces that energy every moment. You have to be wide awake when you immerse yourself in that energy. I know I can't say to you " don't participate" or let that vibration into your space. But I can say, " notice how it makes you feel about yourself and your own life". If it's not feeding a positive vibration, then it's feeding something else and its your job to be ever vigilant about what you swallow not only through your mouth, but also through your eyes.

The important questions are not "am I pretty enough; am I skinny enough; are my boobs big/small enough; am I tall/short enough. The questions should be " am I healthy, am I strong; am I kind; am I generous". When our culture makes those attributes attractive and desirable, we will have won ourselves back from the beast that is the media. And that all begins with you. And me. We must claim our minds back from the machine that has been plugging away at our sense of self for generations. If we don't stand up and notice how our thoughts are influenced and damaged by the perceptions fed to us, we will continue to waste our most precious commodity of life... Time. Time to make a difference. Time to do something that matters. Something that will transform lives and impact our world. .

Think about it. Who gets to decide what size pants validate your body as beautiful and miraculous; or make you valuable enough; and whoever is deciding that, why is anyone listening? We decide by what we agree to believe. You get to be in charge of your mind, but only if you decide to. And if you don't decide to and instead listen to the messages you hear, then you will not be in charge at all. You will have given control to an entity that only cares about money. You hating your body is all about money... about the books you will buy; the medicines you will take; the doctors you will go to to operate on you; the clothes you will buy to prove to someone that you are valuable.

Remember always, that beauty, true beauty is not an outside job. It's an inside job. It's who you are; it's how you treat others, it's how you show graciousness to strangers, it's how you accept others for who they are, it's absolutely how your light shines out into the world. I promise you that it is not the size of your jeans; the size of your butt; the perfection of your make up.

I love you....

Mom

Alaina Reichwald, March 2014

BE A RAINBOW

"You may not control all the events that happen to you, but you can decide not to be reduced by them. Try to be a rainbow in someone else's cloud. Do not complain. Make every effort to change things you do not like. If you cannot make a change, change the way you have been thinking. You might find a new solution."

— Maya Angelou in her letter to her daughter

Dearest Daughter,

When I was given the opportunity to be a part of this wonderful collection of letters, I thought of many letters I would like to write to you. I thought of many different phases of life that I'd like to write them. I pictured us together: you as infant, you as toddler, you as girl, you as teen (now). I pictured all the wonderful moments we have had together. I pictured all the wisdom you already have, wrapped up in you like a rich tapestry, and then I thought "what would I like to add to that?" What do I want to give you at this age that you can carry with you for a long time? And then I pictured us in the future: for some reason we're sitting face to face at a small outdoor table in a cafe, in a village in France or Italy, and we're laughing, sharing, talking, still teaching each other things. "So what do I want to tell her ("future you") right now?" I decided on some things that I feel are really important:

checking in with yourself honestly, being a rainbow, and living life to its fullest.

Check in with yourself honestly. Feel life's up and downs: feel your feelings, both good and bad, and then be honest with yourself, if you don't like something, make a change. Life is not static, its totally DYNAMIC. You can do anything. ANYTHING. So, as far as all those good - nay, GREAT moments in life, oh wow - go with it honey!! Celebrate, laugh, dance, jump for joy, embrace gratitude, hug, high five, smile first, don't hold back. You deserve it. If we highlight and rejoice the good in life, more of it comes our way. MORE OF IT COMES our way. And with the sad, down, bad feelings: you don't have to stay there for long, but its so important to check in with you, take your own emotional temperature, and recognize your true feelings. I have sometimes (don't call me crazy) made myself "greet the feeling" by saying "hello" to sadness, to anger, to confusion, whatever. You are not your feelings. You are your actions. But if you don't know how you feel about something, your actions will most certainly betray you. So know how you feel, what you think, where you stand....because then you will not only end up being honest with yourself, but also liking where you land. By the way, this is not necessarily daily or even weekly: you may only need to "take your emotional temperature" when you're feeling

52

confused about how you feel, which could be rare. The point is: don't be afraid to feel it, and be honest with yourself, then move on.

Live life to its fullest! Travel, be open to new people/places/things, don't let fear hold you back, smile at strangers, assume the best, try your hardest, trust in yourself, and go for it girl!

Traveling opens windows, doors, minds, and souls. I cannot tell you enough how much I implore you to travel every chance you get. Travel when you're young, right out of college, for a few years (or on and off for several years until you're at least 30, and then even if you're settled down, make a life with your love that includes travel!) Try all kinds of places, see the world, make friends, learn to see life through completely different lenses. Dive into the unknown! Bring home what you learn. The world is one: we are one people, a global society, global economy, global consciousness. Most importantly, when you are traveling give people a chance.

Know and embrace diversity: rich, poor, black, white, brown, walking on 1, 2, or no legs, "successful," struggling, speaks 10 languages, can't speak at all, smiles readily, or closed up like an oyster shell. Seek out the one who looks lonely, needs a friend, or – conversely - has made himself/herself the negative but influential power-monger. Be the social lubricant that opens the situation up. Take chances with others: stay safe (obviously), but if you have the chance to talk to someone who you don't normally interact with, be the door opener. Instigate a new friendship with that person who comes from a totally different background from you, or at least who you THINK does. This is SO important.

Work for change, work with the assumption that everyone is waking up and doing the best they can. Positive begets positive. This must be scientifically provable because in my life, I sure feel it. If I put out positive energy, that is what I get back, no matter what background the person comes from. Truly all it takes sometimes is just looking someone in the eyes, being just human, assuming the best, smiling, and taking the time.

LAUGH every single chance you get. Don't take anything too seriously, ever. If you can't think of something funny, think harder. Or just laugh. Laughter brings more laughter. It's contagious and catching. Sometimes we can't laugh. Then: rest. There is always a brighter day tomorrow. So sleep, give yourself the gift of rest and self-care. Your body is your temple, nourish it with rest, water, nutrition, sun, love and laughter.

EACH DAY do something mental, physical, and spiritual. I think these are the three sides of humanity, and each day should reflect that. It doesn't have to be big AT ALL. For example, reading one page of a good book could be the mental bit for the day. You might have days where that's all you have time for. Physical? A short walk can be a complete attitude changer. And spiritual? Well, we could go on a long time here with examples but suffice to say engaging in a spiritual moment runs the gamut for me from smiling at a stranger who looks sad, to skiing perfect powder, to prayer and meditation. There is no script or training manual here; to me being spiritual is just an opening up to a being or power or energy much much greater than yourself. And knowing you are never, ever alone. My prayer for you is that you find a strong spiritual path of your own.

My darling wonderful daughter, everywhere you can be - every chance you get - be a rainbow. Smile. Give to others. Ask how they are. Look in their eyes. Take the time. Take the time. There is no greater gift, than the gift of selflessness. And in selflessness we find fulfillment: total, complete, rich fulfillment.

Love,

Mom

Jenny Fellows Winter, 2013-2014

DO AS I SAY, NOT AS I DO

"There are risks and costs to action. But they are far less than the long range risks of comfortable inaction."
— John F. Kennedy

"In for a penny, in for a pound." "If wishes were horses, beggars would ride." Our house is full of clichés. I admit it, I rarely have an original thought. But I figure these sayings have staying power because they are valuable. They floated around my house growing up along with pearls of wisdom such as, "It's better than a kick in the ass with a club foot" and "It's just as easy to marry a rich man as a poor one." But there is just one that seems to ring in my head every day and that I think are words to live by. You know what it is. It is always preceded with, "You know what your great-great grandmother used to say..." And the response is always the same, "It's never wrong to do the right thing."

Big or small, this adage can get you through any ethical challenge. Need to return a phone call to someone you don't really want to talk to? Committed to going somewhere you don't want to go? Made a promise, but want to break it? I hope these words echo in your head. Want to lie or cheat or help yourself to something you haven't bought or earned? "Remember what your great-great grandmother used to say..."

Sounds so easy. But I know it's not. I struggle with it every time an issue arises. "Shut up!" I want to yell at that voice in my head telling me what to do. "Let someone else be the one to do the right thing for once. Does it always have to be me? I don't want to!" Why are such simple words so hard to follow? I guess because they make us feel uncomfortable and accountable. And the justifications for not doing what we don't want to do are always plentiful and convincing. But these words are the difference between being a stand up gal and being just like everyone else. Look around. How many people do you see cutting corners, not fulfilling obligations, looking the other way when an injustice is being committed?

My wish for you, daughter is that you will always be the one who does what is right. The person who sticks up for the underdog, takes on the bigger challenge, helps someone even when it's inconvenient. It's never easy. It's sometimes messy and always going to be something you wish you didn't have to do. But remember what your great-great grandmother used to say and let the words guide you to always do the right thing.

Jody Rubel, December 2013

SUPERNOVA

"I think that we are like stars. Something happens to burst us open; but when we burst open and think we are dying; we're actually turning into a supernova. And then when we look at ourselves again, we see that we're suddenly more beautiful than we ever were before!"

— C. JoyBell C.

My Beautiful Girls,

Supernova... A blindingly bright star bursts into view in a corner of the night sky — it wasn't there just a few hours ago, but now it burns like a beacon. That bright star isn't actually a star, at least not anymore. The brilliant point of light is the explosion of a star that has reached the end of its life, otherwise known as a supernova. Supernovas can briefly outshine entire galaxies and radiate more energy than our sun will in its entire lifetime. That, my lovelies, is what happens in the souls of humans. It is a natural occurrence for all things. Everything changes. It just does. We fight the idea of change because in change there is an unknown. The unknown is uncomfortable. The idea that change creates a more beautiful you is something I want for you to carry all your life. It is not an idea that I set forth in your hearts from the beginning because I did not come to understand it until very recently.

I grew up with the idea that change was scary. I grew up believing that pain and grief were not to be spoken of. A picture of perceived perfection was cultivated in MY mind as a girl. That perceived perfection created a sense of security for everyone in my family. My father was like the Sun. My mother, brother, sister and I like the planets. The tenor of the family revolved around him and for my father, change was feared. If each of us followed our orbit, then there was peace and harmony in the solar system. I quickly learned my role in the context of my family... all of us did. I was the good girl, the pleaser and the one who made everything all right. I was the Earth, the planet that sustained life. My younger sister was Saturn. She blended into the background staying away from the Sun, far from its heat even if it meant sacrificing its warmth. My brother, Mercury, felt the intense heat of the Sun on one side and the bitter cold on the other. My mother, well, she was Venus; named for the goddess of beauty and love and believed to have once sustained life, she sacrificed much of who she was in order to maintain harmony. We all loved each other, but our roles were our roles. As a girl, I felt safe. I knew exactly how to behave. I watched my brother test different paths and each time it was met with anger, fear and confusion. It caused the whole solar system to break down. So I stayed on track in order to create a bright spot in a sea of uncertainty.

I have carried this way of being most of my life, controlling my environment with happiness. I searched for all things good and closed the door on things that created unrest, even if it meant sacrificing my truths. I came across to all as a girl and a woman that had it all put together while on the inside,I screamed for the need for being accepted and honored for the insecure, messy, childish, frightened person that I was. Because I had learned so early on that my role was being a lightening rod for the happiness of others, I gave up on the notion that I could love myself any other way. I realized that my ability to create happiness through nurturing, honoring and compassion for others as my identity. It made me a wonderful student, daughter, employee, friend, wife and mother. But it also held me back in many ways. I didn't take chances that I should have. I left jobs that I was good at. I poured myself into being perfect at the things that I felt I could be good at, like mothering and being a spouse. I dove into being a good athlete. I tried on many hats but I never wanted to expose myself to criticism for fear that I might be found out as needy or incapable. I tested the waters along the way, showing bits and pieces of fallibility. Much of the time, I felt cast aside for those moments. I truly felt that unless I was perfect, I was unworthy of love. I only felt honored when I was good and right and happy. So I lived in fear of my own emotions and needs. It was not fun. I hid from it. I turned away from compassionately loving myself. It was exhausting and one day I looked up and I felt the sun on my face... So I looked at it... and I realized that change was imminent and that I could no longer hold myself to the standard of perfection I had fought so hard to create. I wanted more for myself. I wanted more for my heart. I wanted to love myself entirely and I wanted to grow beyond the scared little girl clinging to the idea that I was somehow less deserving than anyone else. Thus the beginning of my supernova.

It was violent and many of those around me could not understand. The pendulum swung hard. I lost all sense of who I was. I couldn't see beyond my grief. The grief felt old, ancient really. It was as if I was trying to fix every moment that I sacrificed myself as daughter, wife, but most importantly as a woman. I could not see who I was if I had big, huge emotional change in front of me. How would I recover? Who would I become? Who would love me? What kind of mother could I be if I had my own needs for growth? Where was the lightening rod for my change, my growth, my supernova? So I pushed everyone away... hard. It was lonely and frightening. It was wobbly and violent. I had to come to terms with some terrible things that had happened to me. I had to own my own feelings. I had to accept that I wasn't perfect and that I was not entirely happy. I had to own EVERY part of myself. I had to tell the truth. I had to tell my story. I had to, for the first time in my life, put myself first. I wanted to run away from it so much that it nearly killed me. Ever so slowly, the droning need to honor myself entirely was a beacon. In all of the fear of change, I somehow knew that doing so would make me a better mother and ultimately a better woman and human. I lost the trust and respect of many, especially you, my children, for I painted a picture that was perfect when it was not. When it all came crashing down, you felt betrayed and alone. Those where the moments when the beauty in change was almost impossible to see. I continue to fight my way back from the heartache you endured as a result of the explosion of heart. How I wished that I had not done to you, what was done to me. I wished that I had showed you that things change and that discomfort and change ARE a part of life. How I wished that I would not have insulated you from my pain and fear by trying to craft a perfect world for you. If I had known better, I would have set you up for being ready to face the real world. I used to think that was the harshest attitude. I now understand that the harshest thing to do is to not trust that you have the ability to adapt and understand; because you do and so do I.

Then it happened...slowly. As I began to own my true self, I committed to never hiding it again regardless of what anyone thought about it. I grounded myself in emotional realism and

I brought you with me. I now shield you from little. If I am sad, I say so. If I am scared, I let myself be. The same for anger, fear, resentment, jealousy, and childishness. I show you. I have to, because every one of us IS at one point or another. Without the darkness there is no light. How can we expect anyone to feel joy and love if they never experience hurt, loss and pain? I can say from experience, some of my most joyous moments have come in these past few years and it is because I am learning the art of accepting uncertainty. Those moments presented themselves in very tough conversations with you. One of the most pivotal was looking you in the eyes and letting you share your fear, hurt and betrayal towards me with an open heart and empathetic ear. I held a space for your feelings without judgment. That changed everything about my ability to face criticism and still love myself. If you do it right, you will have many celestial explosions in your lifetime. In its time, each experience will give birth to a new feeling of beauty and strength.

Change comes to you in many forms. You will change jobs, schools, towns where you live. You'll get new cars, pets, and haircuts. Hell, you will certainly change style over the years. Those will be easier to walk through. The changes that will bring you the most growth will be the ones that involve your heart, your emotional path, your past, your future. It will look like loss. It will be cloaked in fear. Real change is about your soul. It will occur at moments where you break free of patterns that chain you to the idea that you have to keep doing things the same way over and over even if it results in seemingly tragic consequences at the moment of implosion. Everything that happens in your life is preparing you for a moment that has yet to come, for those moments that you decide that you WILL NOT walk down the same emotional path you always have. I will not lie to you and tell you that it is something that you learn and it becomes easy. Change is not easy. I have to lean into it every single day.

I am still learning the skills. I fall back into old ways constantly. But the trick is loving yourself even when you fall. At the end of the day, I do not want to be perfect. I don't want to show you a woman that always has it right or has it all going on. I want to show you how to adapt. I want to show you how to grow. I want you to see that facing changes, making mistakes, and being imperfect is the road to self love. Change, my loves... lean into it.

In an effort to allay some of those fears as you face change in your life here are some ideas that I want you to hold with you:

1. *Love yourself first.* You must. Putting yourself first

never means that you are leaving others behind. Real happiness does not come from what is happening around you. It comes from the change that happens inside you. Let it happen. Honor it. Accept it just as the universe itself does.

2. *Don't just listen to what people say. Watch what they do.* The same goes for yourself. Don't listen to self talk that is negative. Look at who and what you really are. Therein lies the most importance.

3. *You don't drown by falling in water. You drown by but knowing how to get out.* ALWAYS challenge yourself to examine different ways to do everything. There are always options. Just because you have walked the same trail over and over does not mean that it is the best trail.

4. *If you don't like something, change it.* If you can't, then change your perspective of it. That takes time and self love to do.

5. *If you expect the world to be fair to you all the time, you will be very disappointed.* Think of this. It is like expecting a lion not to eat you because you didn't eat him. Would that be fair? Sure. But it is not natural.

6. *Things will happen that you don't want to accept but you will have to.* There will be lessons to learn that you don't

want to learn but there will be no other option other than to learn them. There will be people that you love that you will have to let go of in order for the universe to present to you your real purpose and meaning. It will be okay. Quite frankly, it will be beautiful.

7. *Someone else does not need to be wrong in order for you to be right.* When you chose to criticize and judge others it only means that there is something in them that you wish to criticize about yourself but are too afraid to own. Look at what those things are for yourself and own it as part of you. Then change it if you can and honor those less fortunate to be able to do so.

Love,

Mom

Karen Caton, 2014

THE UNIVERSE BEGINS WITH YOU

"Do what you can, where you are, with what you have"
— Theodore Roosevelt

"Light tomorrow with today"
— Elizabeth Barrett Browning

To my beautiful daughter,

There are too many things I want to say to you and share with you; all the things I love about you, the things I'm proud of you for, the things I wish for you, the lessons I've learned that might help you avoid mistakes, but my words would fill too many books. Instead, I've simplified my words in to this poem which is meant to encompass the gamut of my thoughts.

The infinite universe, an infinitesimal grain of sand Your soul, entrusted to me, in the safety and darkness, enters the world: perfect, beautiful, innocent

Into the light, shine your light bright upon this world.

Don't hide it, don't cover it up

Be still, listen to YOUR soul, connect inward with YOU Take the world out of you and put you in the world, don't let the noise confuse you

You are balance, whole like the universe, the "good" and the "bad"

Embrace and have compassion for every part of you Feel the joy and pain, taste the sweet and bitter, experience success and failure Let your passions guide you, keep gratitude in your heart

Enjoy the ride as you let go, surrender

Believe in yourself, feel your power

You are infinite and infinitesimal

You are surrounded by LOVE

With soulful, infinite love from me to you Love,

Mom

Katie Pruski, 2014

ON HONESTY, RESPECT AND MANNERS

"Respect for ourselves guides our morals; respect for others guides our manners"

— Laurence Sterne

Dear Daughters,

Life is full of hope, surprises, joy, stress, sadness, losses, ups and downs. Being a teenager is one of the hardest times of most people's lives, yet I want to let you know that somehow everything really does work out, even if, in a moment, it seems impossible. On the road to working out, there are a few traits that can help you navigate this time and steer you towards spectacular outcomes. They are: Being Honest, Being Respectful, and having Outstanding Manners.

Be honest. It makes life so much easier when you are faced with constant peer pressure and having to make those tough choices. Honesty is not a common trait but it creates trust in every relationship. The friends you hang out with define you, so choose wisely. You need to listen to that voice inside you...your gut instinct is rarely wrong. I want you to be the best person you can be in life so you have lots of options throughout your lifetime. Be the person you would like to have as a friend.

Be aware of others and their feelings and take care of

yourself and your family and friends.

Respect yourself and others. Respect is something that you need to earn. And respect is something tough to get back once you lose it. We all have role models in our lives that we strive to be like and the bar should be set high. For example, you may think of your "Pa" when you define the true meaning of respect and the major impact he had on your lives and so many others. Pa always truly cared about every family member and his friends..he was a true gentleman and was the best listener and seemed to give advice only when it was necessary and one needed to hear it. Carry that with you in your heart.

Manners never go out of style! "Please" and "Thank you" go a long way. Remember that- even if it seems so simple - no matter how old you are manners have a powerful effect on the people you come into contact with. More doors will open for you and more opportunities will come your way.

Stay positive and have faith that things do actually work out how they are meant to in life. Smile often and be friendly. This small touch can truly help make someone's day and in turn you will feel more positive and have a better outlook on life. Eye contact especially with adults is a very important tool you can use throughout your life especially with Teachers,

Coaches, Grandparents and Bosses. It shows respect and that you are interested in what others have to share. Make good choices throughout your life and give yourself the best opportunities that you can. Be honest, respect yourself and others, and don't forget your manners! I love you with all my heart and soul to the moon and beyond!

Xxxooo Mom

Keri Rothhouse, 2014

COLLEGE BOUND

"Twenty years from now you will be more disappointed by the things that you didn't do than by the ones you did so. So throw off the bowlines. Sail away from the safe harbor. Catch the trade winds in your sails. Explore. Dream. Discover."

— Mark Twain

Dear Daughter,

On your first day of college, as you begin this next significant phase of your journey, there are a few things I want to say. If I have done my job adequately these past 18 years, you already know these things, but my hope is that this letter will serve as an important reminder as well as a source of comfort in the coming days, weeks, months and years.

First, and most important, for this is the foundation of everything else: know you are deeply loved and cherished, now and always. In difficult times, this will be hard for you to see so let it be an anchor that tethers you to who you really are and keeps you from going too far astray. In happy times, let it be the soft warm wind that gives you the support and encouragement to soar even higher. So many people love and adore you, in so many different ways and for countless reasons. Stop, occasionally, to see yourself as they do and find all those same reasons to love yourself as well.

Next, do no harm. This is part of the Hippocratic oath doctors take, but whether you pursue that path or not it's a worthwhile promise to keep every day. As you move through your campus and life, you will find yourself in a constantly changing wild and wonderful mixture of people, situations, moods, levels of rest and fatigue, stress and relaxation. Everyone around you will be on this same roller coaster. At times you will share a thrilling, joyful ride; at times you will collide. So tread softly with an abundance of love and compassion for yourself and other. Be ever mindful of your words and actions and always choose the path of kindness and respect. That said, there will be times when you simply feel you can't. In those situations, it's best to simply remove yourself either physically or energetically from the situation. Deep breathing or music helps; "I forgive..." is a powerful mantra.

Another key strategy in both life and the desire to do no harm is to keep an open mind and heart. Be curious, ask thoughtful questions, seek to understand, and look for the positive. Here's the tricky part: do your best to refrain from judgment or attaching to how someone or something shows up. If you find yourself there, try to go back to curiosity. You will find true patience and make fascinating discoveries when you cultivate a sense of wonder and appreciation.

This all sets the stage for you to be bold, to question your own definitions of yourself up to this point and to experiment with new definitions. Perhaps in addition to being an athlete, you are also an artist; in addition to being a student, you are also a teacher; in addition to being highly social, you are also a deep thinker. The possibilities lay before you like a grand and delicious buffet so try a little bit of everything, then go back for more of what you love. And pace yourself :-)

Use passion as your guide. Look for the "hell yes" reaction and follow that trail for awhile to see where it leads. Your passions are the truest indicator of the gifts you uniquely have to give, and it is your moral and spiritual obligation to do so. This is also where you will find profound joy and fulfillment as this is where your most authentic self lives.

Finally, stay connected to your true self by cultivating a strong and personal relationship with God (or whatever name you choose to use). Come to know, not just believe, that you are an individual point of divine consciousness that is from, of, and forever connect to that fundamental source of love. When you begin to understand the vast implications of this, you will also know how deeply and permanently you are loved, that you have nothing to fear (ever), and ultimately there is nothing you can do wrong.

Mom

Kristi Schaffner, 2014

MANIFEST WITHIN

"Whatever you're thinking about is literally like planning a future event. When you're worrying, you are planning. When you're appreciating you are planning. What are you planning?"

— Abraham-Hicks

"Whether you think you can, or you think you can't-you're right"

— Henry Ford

Dear Daughters,

Remembering back on my visions and feelings about you before you were born started me thinking of the way in which other fledgling ideas and feelings shaped my life. Please know that I am writing about what I have taken from my experiences, and also what I have been able to learn from wise teachers.

I have come to a view of existence and creation, which makes sense to me but doesn't always jibe with what others in our culture believe. My first clear experience of this concept came to me after a friend introduced me to some teachings from Abraham-Hicks (AH) about attracting what you want in life. They say it simply,

"That which like unto itself is drawn."

Our 'vibration' is always emanating out from our non-physical self. Some refer to our vibration as our soul, or spirit. By virtue of this 'vibration', similarly vibrating results are brought to us. Our non-physical self chooses a life form to inhabit in order that it may experience the richness of physical existence. How our physical existence evolves is then co-created with an unidentifiable entity they referred to as 'source.' I like this term since 'god', 'creation', and 'universe' all seem so inadequate to describe a higher consciousness we can neither see nor prove. Basically, I believe, our 'vibration' is our non-physical self 'asking for' whatever we are holding in our thoughts and attention, and 'source' is ready and willing to provide it. That might seem extreme, but when we scrutinize our lives, everything we are, have or do always begins with a vibration. For example, remember once when you wanted to see a favorite band in concert, but the show was on a school night, so you just shelved the thought. Then, out of the blue your friend's dad says you are included in a surprise birthday celebration for your friend and he has tickets to that very concert! These kinds of things happen all the time. You could chalk it up to coincidence, but I prefer to believe in using our vibration to create a power of intention.

You'll notice there are associated feelings accompanying these thoughts; excitement, joy, or sadness, etc. When we relish the feeling and savor it, or even just give it our attention, it grows. Eventually we begin to notice external objects and events moving into awareness, which bring to clearer focus what we've been thinking about. At a certain point, fixing attention on it can't be stopped. Pretty soon, it starts to appear as if that 'thing' is everywhere, where before it seemed non-existent. Then the focus intensifies even more. It comes up in conversation, it's talked about, or overheard in public. It's in vivid dreams during sleep. Reminders are noticed on billboards and computer screens. Excitement builds as it is imagined manifesting, coming true. Sometimes it moves into consciousness, sometimes it recedes back into the place of the unseen. Seemingly out of nowhere, we are, have or do exactly what vibration asked for. This is co-creation. We actually get what we wish for! Here's an example; when I was little, I loved being in the kitchen, playing with the tools and the food. I loved the feeling of it. I would watch everything that went on in there. As a teen, I still loved food and all things food related, but helping my mom began to seem more like a chore. I did what was asked of me, but only really got excited about it when it was my ideas I was experimenting with. Since I didn't want cooking to feel like a burden, I started getting creative with it. You know, "switch it up, make it more interesting." Playing mind games got me through it. Then I found it was fun again. Later, when I worked in restaurants, I took what could be perceived as a hard job and turned it into something enjoyable, not just tolerable. I practiced having fun with the public and the staff. I would fantasize about being the owner and how I would implement all of the interesting features I made up in my mind. This mental escapism helped make the time pass, but it also started bringing the likelihood of owning my own restaurant one day that much closer, though I didn't know it at the time.

When an opportunity came to start my own business I jumped in and tried. My first attempt was food related, and I learned a ton, though never made a living at it. My second attempt was focused on artistic creativity using the skills I had with food and running a small business, but again, no luck financially. It was easy to quit when I was making no real money, but I never stopped playing out the fantasy in my mind. When an opportunity to build my own restaurant came up, I never even gave those other experiences another glance, just dove in. The sheer joy and obsession of it really kept me going. I remember not focusing on the outcome, like how much money I would make, but focused on thoughts of how many people would love the food we put out, how the wait staff would treat the guests so they'd come in again and again. What I would put on the menu or which interiors I'd pick. These thoughts energized me. I experienced real success with that venture, none of which could have been possible without the constant 'vibration' of love for it.

You know I don't believe that manifestation, getting exactly what you want, is magic. It seldom happens instantly, or exactly as you envision. I once watched a movie where a young boy attained magic powers. He would have an emotional impulse and whatever it was he wanted, would instantly appear. This was great at first when he could have a new toy, or watch all the TV shows he liked, or eat all the ice cream he could dream of. He was ecstatic and it was cool - at first. Eventually the audience becomes horrified, as the boy gets tired of listening to his sister and wishes she had no mouth, then her mouth is erased. Or he creates a home and furniture straight out of a cartoon that at first is really stylish and cute but then feels 'all wrong,' disturbing even. The boy then eliminates everything resembling mature supervision. His parents disappear. Everything starts to get really creepy. It ended very badly and I don't necessarily recommend the film, but its lessons did stick with me in a palpable way.

No, I don't believe manifestations occur like they did for the boy in that movie. It actually takes a sustained attention to your desire. Paradoxically, a sustained non-attachment to the outcome is important, too. Confusing? Yes and no. You don't need to labor over your desire, just enjoy wanting it. So practice a little 'catch and release.' Get that fantasy or desire swirling in your mind, savor it, love it, and then get back to loving where you're at now and being fully engaged in what you are doing. Soon, you'll be pondering your desire again, loving and refining the feeling of it, and then letting it go. I guess no co-creation comes to pass without that letting go part. It's been essential to me to surrender and practice that lack of expectation that it be a 'certain way.' Very tricky that last bit. I still suffer strong feelings of frustration and discomfort whenever I'd rather be doing, having, or being something else. Non-attachment is all about loving where you currently are and having faith that each moment is exactly as it should be. The sweet dreams of the future should be a playlist running in the background of your mind, not distracting you from the present, but slyly loading your potential with all the good stuff.

An important key point is to have the strength of patience and gratitude for where you currently are. Harbor the trust that the universe will always provide for you. It works wonders. I have seen time and again that you get what you want out of life, often effortlessly. I have also seen you struggle with not having what you want, not liking the feelings you're having, then settling in, detaching from the outcome, accepting where you are, and enjoying what shows up anyway. This is where all of the good stuff is (you are better at all of this than me because you 'go with the flow' more). For this I am deeply relieved and grateful.

When the need for the outcome to be a 'certain way' is released, something miraculous occurs. Visions begin to show up in the physical realm more quickly. Daily reminders of the visions (consciously or unconsciously) surround us. Little glimpses of ideas take hold deep within and the feelings attached to them swell, but without expectation. Then, more and more, this idea begins to manifest into our reality. One day "voila!" we have the true experience of what we set forth.

Visions, dreams, and inspirations are very powerful. You are lucky to have a rich inner life of dreaming, visioning, and imagining. It brings me so much happiness for you. Keep leaning on your inner life to sustain you through the tough times, the times you have tasks to do you're not fond of. It bears repeating that these nonphysical thoughts set the stage for the creative force to bring something to pass. That is why it is so important to be 'pure of intention.' Meaning 'clear' and 'unsullied with conflict.' Even if we have conflicting thoughts within us, if we strengthen the desired imagery, the conflicts begin to fade or resolve. A pure intention is joyful on its own. It makes us feel warm and alive. When we allow ourselves to receive this impulse, we are participating in the flow of creation. Nothing is too far fetched to imagine. Do you desire a particular item? Fantasize about enjoying it. Want to experience peace on earth? Practice pretending that everything is blissful and people are happy. Want to feel loved and cherished? Create the perfect warm glowing scenario in your mind of how you want to be treated.

Imagination is maybe our strongest asset. It is so important to deploy it wisely. Don't fall into the trap of dampening your rich inner life, or arguing for your limitations. Sometimes we convince ourselves that we can't have, or don't deserve, or haven't earned our desires. Notice if you have thoughts like this. How do you feel when you negate an otherwise perfect fantasy? The surest way to stifle creativity is to disallow the joy to be felt. A technique you can use to turn around a negative impulse is to make a mental game of 'what if there were instant manifestation?' Would you still be content to send harsh judgments outward? To yourself? To others? Would you focus on that which you don't want or feel sorry for yourself? Would you feel envious of others? By playing 'What If,' perhaps you can use your energy to better imagine what it's like to instantly create beauty? Or when you witness suffering, you imagine the miraculous resolution of it. These things matter. I wish for you to always cast yourself in the role of the happy manifestor in your mind.

No matter what, always vibrate intense gratitude. It is

possible to project the very best outcome and still be thankful, fulfilled and pleased with your current situation, however much it varies from what you're intending. This is tricky to pull off at first. How can you simultaneously envision a beautiful outcome (even if it doesn't exist outside of your mind) and still be grateful, thrilled and joyous over what is actually occurring here in the physical moment? Focusing on what you want vs. being upset over what is can be a tough habit to form. It is possible, though. Even more than possible, it's imperative that you set your energetic focus on feeling the feelings of the favorable outcome, and sending thanks.

Whatever state of mind you hold is like an order form to the universe to get more of it. Do you want to be surrounded with creative, powerful, active, awake and alive people? Or would you rather be submerged in a group of complaining, negative, victim types? How about feeling alone, unhappy, depressed or self- pitying? You could ask to be alone and be perfectly miserable. Or, you could ask to be alone and be so deliciously content. You might want to be surrounded by lots of friends, or you could ask for only one friend to feel safe with. All of these requests and more are choices, which are available to you. I love the phrase 'infinite possibilities.' There are literally unlimited ways that things can turn out. You'll get whichever ones are held with the most emotional charge in your thoughts and feelings. Remember the story of the two different wolves inhabiting our minds. Which wolf survives? The one you feed.

So what happens when you slip, or develop negative thoughts? Here's another quote about that,

"Just say yes to whatever it is. Because if you say yes to it and then you get in the middle of it, and you say, "Uh oh, this isn't really turning out the way I wanted it to," then out of that is born another desire. And as you say yes to that, then it turns out. And you say, "Well, it's still not quite right." So you have another desire... Until eventually you get it exactly right. You cannot get it wrong. No creation is ever complete. Just do it. Those old habits don't have to be erased, they just become replaced by a new habit that is more in vibrational harmony with who you are and what you want."

So let those thoughts be and move on. And please, in no way spend your time fretting about the future or fearing some imagined event. Do you know the Bobby McFerrin song, "Don't Worry, Be Happy?" It is such a great song to carry around. Here's another great quote by Abraham Hicks,

"Worrying is using your imagination to get that which you don't want"

My dear, beautiful, powerful, sensitive girl please know that I envision the absolute best for you. I hope from these pages, something great will resonate with you. I hope that you will consciously, intentionally and thoughtfully create for yourself a future of your own choosing. You're going to manifest whatever you vibrate, you might as well order up something terrific!

I love you with all of my heart and soul,

Mama

Lauren Reinkens ,2014

LET INTUITION LEAD

"Have the courage to follow your heart and intuition. They somehow already know what you truly want to become."

— Steve Jobs

Dear Daughter,

You are going to be pulled by a strong force within you called your Inner Guidance.

You will know you are headed in the right direction when you are feeling pulled towards something; and you will know you are going in the wrong direction when every part (or even a small part) of your inner self is saying "wrong way". Your work is to begin to listen to that still small voice that is always trying to communicate with you.

What does your inner guidance sound or feel like? It can be a quiet whisper pushing you towards something that you may feel a bit afraid to do.

It can be a nudge of interest in a person, place, situation or course of learning. It can be a feeling when you meet someone... an immediate comfort and familiarity telling you that this person is special. It can also warn you away from potentially toxic or dangerous situations.

As you begin to pay more and more attention to how you body and emotions feel in certain situations, you will begin to grow more and more attuned to that inner guidance. And as you listen more and more carefully, and honor it by following it's lead, it will grow stronger and stronger inside of you.

In my life, my inner guidance has played a central role. Sometimes, I have listened carefully; sometimes it has taken me awhile to take its lead; and other times I have ignored it all together. None of that matters. What matters is knowing what it sounds like; feels like; looks like and how it is reinforced by the world and coincidences that happen around you.

There are no mistakes in life. We may go down a path that is unpleasant, but we also learn and grow from those experiences and they can often help increase our intuition if we notice what happened right before we went down this path. Did we have a subtle feeling that this was not the right choice? Were there signs telling us that we might not enjoy this experience? If we can honestly reflect on even the most difficult and painful situations, we may again discover our intuition was walking right there alongside us and we either didn't recognize it or chose not to follow it.

But never worry, because our Intuition is a steadfast and true companion and never leaves our side. It will be right there waiting for us to pay attention and will still provide reliable information no matter how many times we may have ignored it in the past.

Love,

Mom

Alaina Reichwald, 2015

YOUR INNER SPARK

"One man's candle is light for many"

— *Talmud*

Dear dear Daughter,

You have always been the light of my soul, and indeed, you showed me for the first time what a soul looks like, as I could see your pure one leaping out for cuddles and kindness and caring in your young life. Through you, I have been able to see the beauty in many more people, and can recognize their inner beauty as well.

This inner beauty comes from within our souls, that spark of the divine that each of us has. At the beginning of the Torah, we learn that the Holy One decided to create the human in the image and likeness of the divine spirit and then created that first person in the image only. Clearly we do not look like the Holy One of Blessing – because no one would know what that looks like. We all see holiness differently. You see it as the Great Spirit, I see it as a wave of energy bending the universe toward good, others see an old man with a beard, or the rays of sunlight peering through the clouds. Even the writers of the Torah had no idea what their Elohim or Adonai looked like, and the guys (okay, sages) from the Talmud times talked about the 70 faces of God, because we each perceive that holiness differently.

But the important idea for me is that we are each made in the image of that holiness—that we each have the capacity to act in a holy way. And at the same time, each of us is a unique person endowed and blessed with that spark of holiness. Therefore, how we treat each other, and how we allow ourselves to be treated could reflect our awareness of it.

You, my beloved daughter, are clearly created in the image of holiness, with a soul that shines with goodness. I am sad that you sometimes forget or block out or don't remember your spark as the daughter of royalty (not Daddy and me, but the daughter of holiness). At those times, you let people treat you as less than the princess you are.

If I could have one wish for you, I would wish that you could catch glimpses of your soul, your spark, your inner beauty, and be able to say and act upon and believe in your bones that you deserve to be handled in a way that shows how valuable you are to the world around you, not just to Daddy and me, but to the wider world. After all, there is no one like you, no one born to be the person you are supposed to be, and that makes you precious and worth more than all the jewels in the world. I imagine an orchestra or a dance troupe--

it takes every person to make the music come alive or the dance to be whole. Each member brings their own instrument--whether it is the triangle, the piano or their own body--and each person is essential. The music would sound different, the dance would look different, without each one of us. So when you look at other people, you can try to see what their instrument is, what part they play in our cosmic dance. So let no one walk on you, injure you, hurt you, make you think you are "less than". Hold this image of holiness in your heart and draw on it whenever you need strength. Whenever someone tries to make you feel smaller than you really are, tells you "You can't do that," or "You're ....stupid, or fat, or you keep doing the same dumb thing", or tries to physically hurt you--walk away from them as quickly as possibly. Think about whether this is someone you want in your life. If it is someone you think is important, try talking to them about it, and if they still persist, that's a clue that you should leave. Now.

Now let's go back for a moment to the story of the first human's creation. The plan was that the first human would be made in the image and likeness of the Source of All Life, but the final creation was only in the image. What happened to the likeness? Rabbi Rami Shapiro teaches that we have to choose to live in the likeness of the Holy One, by acting as we believe holiness is: caring for the vulnerable, respecting all creatures, taking care of the sick, welcoming the stranger, doing acts of loving-kindness, studying, praying. We need to be the hands, the feet, the kiss, the hug, that other people—also created with the divine spark in the image—need. I know that this is one of your gifts, that you brings gifts to people, and most living things, with your hugs, your love, your attention that people crave. But keeping that responsibility in your mind and your actions will help you keep your soul pure each day. When you go to sleep, in addition to thinking about what you are grateful for, think about what you've done to make the world a better place, and what you need to fix that you might have done. Is there a relationship that needs an apology or a person who needs a check-in conversation? Make a mental note (or even write it down) to do it tomorrow. Is there someone you know who needs help? Is there a way you can give it? While you are so good at this, sometimes you can be more systematic about it.

And finally, I want to return to the idea that you are here as a unique soul with your own task to do. We won't be asked why we weren't more like Moses, but why we were not the best of ourselves that we could have been. I used my wish on wanting you to recognize the worth of your inner spark; but I will still pray every day that you find the path that is yours and you move along it with passion, energy, joy and commitment. Then, when the time comes for that question, you will be able to say, "I did the best I could."

Know that I am blessed to be your mother, and will always recognize the soul that your body cares for.

With all my love,

Mama

Rabbi Meredith Cahn, 2013

OPEN HEARTED VULNERABILITY

"Sensitivity is a sign of life. Better hurt than hardened. I bow to those who keep their hearts open when it is most difficult, those who refuse to keep their armor on any longer than they have to, those who recognize the courage at the heart of vulnerability. After all the malevolent warriors end each other, the open-hearted will inherit the earth."

— Judah Isvaran

My Dear Daughter,

You are beautiful, intelligent, and talented at many things. Sadly, I do not see you much any more. Ours has not been an easy mother daughter relationship. No doubt we are not alone, yet I continue to believe that the differences that have divided us will be healed someday, and we will find a sense of closeness and kinship and perhaps even friendship in the coming months and years. I cannot begin to describe the love I feel for you and the belief I have that you are a complete success. My deepest yearning for you as you travel through life is that you find inner peace and genuine happiness. With this, everything else will fall into place.

You have been my greatest teacher although I will admit I wasn't always the most astute pupil, and I apologize for my mistakes, all of them. A day doesn't pass that I don't wish for a do over. When your teen years knocked at the gate, they did not slip in like a lamb, subtle, gradual and unnoticed. They hit suddenly and unmistakably with the force of a tsunami, a clash of thunder and a bolt of lightening, gale force winds and sheets of rain. You swiftly, decisively and strongly rejected your ties to me, cutting through the umbilical cord of our connection with the machete of your own free choice. Though it broke my heart, I knew I had to let you go, respect your decision and trust that you were taking care of yourself in the best way you knew how. I had to wean you a bit early, like our cat, who we took from her mother earlier than her brother and sister. She turned out alright, and I have to trust that you will, too.

For at least half of your high school years you have made your way without your mother. It wasn't what I had envisioned when you were young. I imagined myself ushering you through the turbulence of the teen years in connection. This is not at all how it has unfolded. Contrary to my vision, you are crossing through the threshold of childhood into adulthood without my active participation. To be sure, I have always been on the sidelines cheering you on and loving you just the same, humbly accepting that I could have no direct influence on your daily life and decisions as a teen.

Soon, you will set sail out into the high seas of the adult world, moving out on your own, making your contribution to our world. I would like to offer my simple, heartfelt advice arising from my own experiences in making the same journey over 40 years ago and from the intimate experience of knowing you and raising you. You can either take it or leave it. Truly, there are no strings or expectations attached, just a few words of humble guidance.

1. Treasure this precious human life you have filled with intelligence, talent, abundance and opportunity. Develop your gifts and use them to make the world a better place for all.

2. The environment is in need of healing. Do everything you can to help our planet and encourage others to do so, as well. Without healing for our planet, all life as we know it will perish under the weight of greed and materialism.

3. Take care of your health: eat a healthy diet, brush and floss your teeth, exercise, get plenty of rest, avoid drugs and alcohol, keep good company, meditate regularly. This will help prevent a great deal of suffering for yourself and others.

4. Get a good education. It is still the best way to be financially successful and independent in the world.

5. Create a rich inner life, an inner wellspring of wellbeing, and go there often for emotional and spiritual nourishment.

6. *Develop compassion for others and help to reduce suffering in the world.*

7. *Look beyond physical appearances. As my mother, your grandmother, said often, beauty is only skin-deep. It is who you are, not what you look like that truly matters.*

8. *Be a skeptic, but be willing to commit to a cause.*

9. *Always know that, despite the difficulties we have encountered, your mother's heart is open and vulnerable patiently waiting for the day of our reconnection and renewal.*

My love for you is infinite,

Mom

Polly Ryan, 2014

RULES ARE MADE TO BE BROKEN

" If you obey all the rules you miss all the fun".

— Katharine Hepburn

Katherine Hepburn enjoyed a rich life in a time when men made all the rules about how women should behave. She was a fiercely independent woman who questioned the validity of commonly held ideas. Determination and a relentless belief in her own judgment led her to challenge society's expectations and to live a passionate life with a stellar acting career and true love. She was a scandalous rule-breaker...and a happy one. In the radical style of this powerful woman, I offer you three ideas for consideration.

Question Authority.

Holding a position of authority doesn't naturally make someone an expert. Question everyone, all the time. Do it out loud or even just inside your own head. Parents, families, teachers, news reporters, bloggers, advertisers, fashion magazine editors – they all have their own agendas. Question what you hear in relation to what you already know to be true about the world, about yourself, about what you value. You are the authority in your life, the director of your own life's story. When you allow your innate sensibility, your intellect, your inner voice, to guide you to heed or disregard what others tell you to do, is true, must be, then you control the forces that shape your inner landscape. Be sure you are the one holding the reins to your life. To hand them over is to abdicate a beautiful right to navigate your own marvelous journey.

Now, I'm not suggesting you never listen – on the contrary – listen closely and with full attention when authority speaks. Think actively, why am I compelled to listen to this? What credentials does this person have? From what experiences does it speak? Learn from those who have had experiences different from your own, been places you have yet to visit. Glean gems of wisdom, new ideas, and be open to new truths. Select the relevant ones and weave them into your own story. Listen with your whole self, hear what is behind the spoken word and decide what is true for you. And if their truth is not for you, makes you squirmy or uncomfortable, is harmful to anyone, is based on greed or avarice, well then, move on. Either walk away from it, work around it, or actively rail against it!

Question the Rules.

All the time, in every situation in which you are asked to make decisions, question the validity of the rules. Think actively. Why were they deemed necessary? For whom were these rules designed? Am I a member of that group? If the rules make sense to you, if they offer protection to you or others, if they feel necessary, by all means follow them...until they don't. Then make your own. You will find some rules work for you for a time and then need adjusting, or overhauling, or even tossing. You are constantly growing and changing in mind, body, and spirit - wouldn't you expect to outgrow some rules?

Reevaluate the structures in your life and ask yourself if they are still effective. We operate inside the rules for good reasons. Taking a series of classes in school builds a solid foundation for future learning so we can pursue our interests. Driving inside the designated lines prevents traffic chaos and creates safety. Writing and speaking with proper grammar facilitates precision in communication, and following rules of social etiquette develops stronger community and personal relationships. Those are powerful guideposts with purpose. But operating from outside a structure of rules can also have purpose. Retail stores bag your merchandise in products that create trash in landfills and pollute our planet. Until 1972, college sports teams were only open to men. Until 1920, only men were allowed to vote. What rules in your world are no longer useful? Are the once helpful guideposts now restrictive fences? Throw out the rules that block you from spectacular experiences!

Which leads me to my final bit of advice.

Question Your Choices.

Say yes... and often! Say yes to experiences when they present themselves– they may not come again. Say yes even if it breaks the "rules". Think actively, am I missing an opportunity to grow because I'm choosing to follow an arbitrary rule? Will I be better, wiser, or stronger for my choice? You aren't really obligated to do most anything in life – you only have to be willing to accept the consequences of your choices. Say yes to the things that evoke a passion in your being! Say yes to an opportunity to travel, to volunteer, or to demonstrate for a cause. Say yes to a break-up, a new relationship, a job opportunity - even if it goes against the flow, even if it is not the expected path, even if your parents, teachers, friends might disapprove! If your choices are thoughtful, cause no harm to yourself or others, then the only approval you need is the voice inside you. Just because your family or friends have always celebrated a holiday, voted a political agenda, followed a specific diet, doesn't mean you have to. Make your own traditions, or have none at all!

Sometime the most enriching experiences or life-altering moments exist in direct opposition to the established expectations. Rules can be meaningful, reasonable and protective. But the experiences we have when we test others' limits are the ones that enable us to discover who we are in times of turmoil, anxiety, joy, and excitement. They stretch the fabric of who we think we are and present us with personal insight, enrich our being, lead us to become our most interesting and complex selves. Occasionally and intentionally stepping past the " No Trespassing" signs may reveal undiscovered treasure, both literally and figuratively. So in your journey to become the best version of yourself, I wish for you a lifetime of moments where you break some of the rules, say yes, and have some of the fun!

Love,

Mom

Reenie McMains, 2014

DON'T WORRY, YOU CAN FIGURE IT OUT

Ask yourself this question:
"Will this matter a year from now?"
-Richard Carlson, Don't Sweat the Small Stuff
"Be yourself; everyone else is already taken."

— Oscar Wilde

My dearest daughter:

When I was asked what advice I would give to my teenage daughter to help make the next few years of her life a little easier, my first thought was to say, "Don't worry; it'll all work out." But after some more thought, my advice is, "Don't worry, take action instead, and then accept the outcome and move on."

Anyone who knows me knows that I am not much of a worrier; so of course, when I see my beautiful, teenage daughter stressed about something, it is hard to watch. I wonder why some people worry and others don't. And then I wonder if it's possible to teach someone how to worry less. So I thought I'd give it a try.

My suggestion is this: If you are worrying about something, think about what is bothering you, then figure out what you can do to change the situation that is causing you stress. In other words, identify the problem and then do something to resolve it.

For example, are you worried that a boy you like doesn't like you? The problem here is that you like him but you don't know if he likes you. So why not find out if he likes you? You can ask him if he likes you, have a friend ask him, or maybe even tell him that you like him. Confronting that situation directly should solve the problem of not knowing. But those options may sound too bold or aggressive for your personality. So now, maybe the answer to your problem is that you have to find a way to accept that you don't know if he likes you. Finding a way to live with the unknown may not be what you wanted, but it is sometimes the answer to reducing your worrying about all sorts of topics. In other words, accept that you don't know if he likes you.

Another example would be that you are worried that you're not going to do well on a test. I say, instead of worry about it, take some action. An action would be to study more or to ask for help if there's something in the material you don't understand. But what if you're worried because you don't have time to study more; than what? This is a case when you may just have to accept that you have done all that you can. Try to relax, focus on what you know and then do the best you can. Once the test is over, regardless of how well or poorly you may have performed, accept the results and then move on. I am a firm believer that you learn from your mistakes. Once the test is over, it is in your past, so don't dwell on things you cannot change.

One more example: Are you worried that your friends have a bad influence on you? You may be wondering, "What can I do about that?" My advice is to re- evaluate who you're hanging out with. Ask yourself, "Why am I spending time with this person? Do I really like them? Do I have things in common with them or are they just someone I've known for a long time?" Decide if you want them to be your friend and then take action.

To recap, my advice is "don't worry, take action instead," and my approach is "identify the problem and then do something to resolve it." In a few of my examples, I also said that sometimes, accepting something is all you can do and that it's okay to make mistakes since we often learn from our mistakes. It is important to remember that certain things are out of our control.

So, step one is to identify the problem. How do you identify the problem? To start, just think about it. Ask yourself, "What is bothering me?" I call this "listening to your inner voice;" or "having a conversation with yourself." I have found that there are certain times of the day or certain places where I can think more clearly than others. For example, I often do my best thinking in the shower. And I think pretty clearly when it's quiet and I'm not distracted. So, figure out if you need to turn off the music, go for a walk, or sit in the backyard. Another way I work towards identifying a problem is I get a piece of paper or sit down at my computer and start writing my thoughts down. Sometimes, just by writing down what's bothering me, I get it out of my head and I can stop thinking about it for a while. And sometimes, after I finish the conversation with myself, I realize that I'm letting something bother me that shouldn't and it's as simple as that....it goes away. And then there are times when I realize that I need to do something about the problem.

Step two- Take action. Sometimes the action needed is to just let some time pass. Waiting a few days can be all you need for a problem to go away. The reason it can be helpful to write down what is bothering you is because (1) there are times when just writing it down makes you feel better and (2) there are times, when a few days have passed, and you look back at what it was you were thinking and you realize that it really wasn't as big of a problem as you thought. Time often gives you perspective on what is important and what isn't. Of course, problems don't always go away just because time has passed, but I think you'll be surprised by how often the problem seems easier to solve once you've had time to think about it or to get some perspective. So, when you do have to take action, how do you decide what to do? Of course, the answer to that will depend on the issue you are having. It is often helpful to ask for help from your parents, trusted adult or trusted friend. But what will serve you well for a lifetime is for you to learn to trust yourself. With each problem that you resolve, your confidence will grow and you will realize that you can rely on your own strength and intelligence to solve your problems. You should face each issue with an open mind, be honest with yourself about what is bothering you and what you think will be a good solution for you and those involved.

Again, the advice is to identify the problem which can be done by listening to your inner voice, having a conversation with yourself or writing down what's bothering you. You may never have tried writing down your thoughts before; and while it sounds simple, you might find yourself staring at a blank piece of paper or a blank computer screen wondering what to write. So here are some examples; write: "I am sad because....," I am frustrated because.....," I felt lonely at lunch today because no one was talking to me." Once you are able to identify how you feel and what the event was that led to your feelings, it should be easier to figure out how to stop letting it bother you or stop worrying about it. Maybe you yelled at a friend today. You may want to call that friend and apologize or when you see that person at school the next day let them know that you are sorry for yelling at them. You could explain to them why you did it (i.e. I was just in a cranky mood yesterday or I was annoyed at my mom from the morning so I took it out on you, etc.) or just leave it at a simple apology. Clearing the air with friends almost always makes you feel better and helps your friendships grow stronger.

And now here are some random things to consider that may help you navigate through your adolescent years: There are times when you just need to take your mind off things. Instead of listening to music or watching tv, consider pulling out old photo albums of yourself or your parents. Or start compiling a list of sayings you like or that are meaningful to you. Keep the list somewhere convenient and read it when you need a little boost in your mood. I like simple sayings; a few of the ones I think are helpful for stressed teenagers are "This too shall pass" and "Forgive and forget."

Try to focus on the positive and to keep a positive attitude.

Sometimes just a little patience and understanding make things better. Forgiveness and acceptance are helpful skills to have.

And don't forget to forgive and accept yourself; don't be too hard on yourself or too critical of yourself. Try to be realistic about your strengths and weaknesses. Embrace your strengths and either accept or work on your weaknesses.

Developing these skills takes time, practice and lots of patience to develop. Those who love to "take action" can struggle taking time to see if something resolves without action. And some prefer to sweep things under the rug in hopes they will go away, and taking action will be the most difficult. Know what your tendencies are and see those tendencies in the middle of a challenge... and then ask, what would be best here for me. lifetime to figure it out!

Love,

Mom

Susie Harris December, 2013

BE COURAGEOUS ENOUGH TO BE YOU

"Life shrinks or expands in proportion to one's courage."

— Anaïs Nin

Dear Daughter,

One of the most valuable lessons I have learned is to be true to yourself. This simple lesson has at times taken more courage than I thought I personally possessed. There have been moments in my life, I could not muster the courage to see what my own needs were and where others needs or even societal pressures were crushing my spirit. I have spent soul-searching hours wondering and even worrying about what I am truly supposed to be doing; want to be doing; and should be doing. I have created a lot in my life and I am grateful that ultimately, I believed in myself. It's been a journey. I have doubted myself, a lot, but now I look forward to every single day. What I will create; learn; how will I be touched and how can I touch others.

I've learned, it all works out, so why not carve out exactly the life that you want for yourself? This can happen when you are courageous enough to be true to yourself. You will wake up feeling grateful and you will feel love around you every day. You will choose to grow on the path that is the one you are on right now because it led you here to these letters.

Letters written by women who have needed guidance too, and, sometimes still do, but who want to share their truth with you as we learned one way or the other along the way. You will make some decisions along the way that you decide need to change; you will make agreements that you have to break; you will fall in love with the wrong people; you will walk away from the right ones. It's all ok. Big decisions, change. Love as well as heart-ache are all a part of life. When you need to make important decisions, gather all the information from those whose opinion you value. Trust that you will gather all the necessary information in order to make those big decisions and then let it all go, and just breathe.

Take time to be alone in order for you to connect to you. Ask yourself if you could do anything, ANYTHING, at all in this situation what would it be? When it feels right, even if it's a huge dream, DO IT!!

To get what your heart desires, it just might take a lot of courage. No matter what be true to yourself. I promise you it's worth it, it's how I got you...my daughter, and all of the other beauty in my life.

In peace,

Tanya Rose Bordner, 2015

THE ROAD LESS TRAVELED

Life should not be a journey to the grave with the intention of arriving safely in a pretty and well preserved body, but rather to skid in broadside in a cloud of smoke, thoroughly used up, totally worn out, and loudly proclaiming "Wow! What a Ride!".

— Hunter S. Thompson

Dear Daughter,

Your family, schooling, community has spent years keeping you within the parameters of a certain box. A cultural societal box, so to speak. You have been taught ways of doing things; ways of learning; ways of everything. Maybe in your mind you have come to believe that these ways are THE ways, the "right" ways. The only right ways.

I hope as you go forward and become more independent you break the mold of the things you are used to doing a certain way and strike out to do things in ways unimaginable. It reminds me of the poem by Robert Frost called The Road Not Taken. "Two roads diverged in a wood and I, I took the one less travelled by, and that has made all the difference". It has been one of my favorite poems since college and I have kept that quote close to me for many many years. I reminds me that just because everyone is going in a certain direction, doesn't mean I'm required to follow. But I have had to realize too, that often since that path is filled with familiarity, I can be called to the comfort of it. Mesmerized, hypnotized perhaps. It can be like falling asleep and waking up years later in a common life realizing that you left adventure at the gate. But truly, the most exciting moments in my life have been when I have taken a less travelled path. When I have gone in a direction where people have looked at me sideways, as if not understanding what I am doing or why I am making the life choices I am.

When I have done these "less common" things, I have never regretted them or wished I had followed the herd. The herd all moves together. When one changes direction, they all change to follow some unseen leader. They trample down the same grass; eat nose to nose; go to the same destinations; eat at the same restaurants; talk about the same things.

Instead, I have made great efforts to go towards my interests and curiosities even knowing that many people would not understand what I was doing. But even more so, having to overcome my own discomfort walking towards the unknown and unfamiliar.

Having come from a herd mentality life myself, there were very few guides who could tell me what I might discover or find. I had to have faith along with the other seekers that the journey would be worth it.

Although people will try to tell you there are all these rules in life, I'm here to remind you that there actually are not. When you think you are supposed to follow a certain direction, ask inside your mind "why". Is it what you want or what you think you are supposed to do.

Begin that dialogue, and amazing things will unravel, and bright unexpected opportunities will come forward. Take them. Be inspired. Be afraid and then be fearless.

Life is our greatest adventure and we only get this one life one time.

Love,

Mom

Alaina Reichwald, 2015

THE POWER OF A SMILE

"A smile is a curve that sets everything straights"
— Phyllis Diller

They say that the eyes are the window to the soul. I believe this. The smile unlocks the window and cracks it open just enough to catch the power of the divine nature of each unique individual. Smiles are free and they help you, along with the person on the receiving end, to feel connected with the universe and the human race. A smile is like a kiss that leaves you bathing in gentle warmth. One good smile can lift you up, lighten your load, and carry you through your day. It is like a shot of espresso. It energizes and grounds us. A smile can break down cultural, economic, racial, and social barriers. It is a blanket of love.

Try smiling at someone and if you are lucky enough to get a genuine smile back you will see, if you pay attention, a flash of light in their eyes. It is as if we can see the Star Energy of the Universe for a fleeting second. The collective wisdom of all mankind. Some people can keep the window open longer than others when they smile. These smiles are SO powerful that they make me gasp for air and send me reeling! When you witness this type of smile it is a remarkable moment. You most likely will remember a beautiful smile from a stranger all day long.

On the other hand, if you go thru the day and too many people are NOT smiling, they can drain your energy and make you feel disconnected like a fading star. Especially if you smile at them and they look away. So why not use your secret powers to make someone's day and be rewarded in kind. Why not light up the universe like a fairy Godmother with a magic wand?

I love to smile and make others smile around me. I tend to make a game of it especially when I see someone not smiling and looking anxious or withdrawn. The reaction I am usually able to get is startling. A huge smile from someone you thought didn't even have it in them is worth the price of admission! I routinely smile at certain groups I feel need it most. Immigrants, the elderly and handicapped, shy and socially awkward kids, and of course children. The key is not feeling better than anyone else. Remember, if you want to live a truly blessed life, it starts within and ends within.

I always smile when I catch eyes with Immigrants because they may feel socially disconnected or at times unwelcome or intimidated in their new land. Try moving to a different country with NO money, little education (which a lot of immigrants unfortunately don't have) and a complete language barrier. A smile to them is like a 1,000 kind warm words. It lets them know it is ok. When an immigrant woman smiles back at me, I see with the spark in her eyes and the white of her teeth that she too knows the ancient universal wisdom handed down to us all. For that one very moment she is not from Africa, Mexico or some distant land, but my sister. One, like me, with the universe. No richer, no poorer, no smarter, no prettier, no better or worse a human than I. Her life experiences may have been different, but she is no different than me.

A smile is universal in its appeal.

Handicapped and Elderly folks need a smile most of all. They have NOTHING compared to the blessings we have! An 87 year old Alzheimer's patient, a person in a wheelchair, or a kid with Down Syndrome still can recognize a smile and feel the love that radiates from it. My elderly mother doesn't know who I am anymore but when my children or I smile at her she smiles back and I see the window to her soul for a brief moment.

One of my good girlfriends paraplegic brother used to attend college with me. I befriended him (or perhaps he befriended me) with the blessing of friendship. We sat outside the classroom waiting for class to start every morning and often times I would join him for lunch. His smile was so bright when he saw me that I felt like a rock star! Nobody else on campus mattered. My friendship brought him a tiny bit of joy and that became my most important mission for the two years we went to school together. I would run over to him all the way across the courtyard before the bell rang just to say hi and make him smile ......then back again to my class. As I ran I realized he had never been able to experience the feeling of sprinting across a courtyard and I was thankful that I had my legs and thankful that I was conscious enough to realize that. For those of you that feel awkward when you see someone old or handicapped, DON'T. Feel blessed you still have your youth, your health and your mind. Smile with genuine compassion and send intentional love to those that don't. Your smile will be well received and the universe will thank you. The handicap and elderly are wise enough to receive your blanket of love and will embrace it with much thanks! Often times that smile may be the only bit of joy they experience all day and you have the power to dispense that joy!

Socially awkward or shy kids could really use a smile from everyone around them letting them know you accept them without judgment. When you feel good inside one cannot help but share the beauty of that feeling and it comes out as a

SMILE! I was one of the rare kids that figured this out at an early age and smiled at everyone in school.

I recommend smiling at everyone. Disarm them with a smile. Who can turn that down. If you smile a genuine smile and someone does not smile back that says a lot about that person. Perhaps THEY have deeper insecurities than you know. If you are secure with yourself, you will smile to the world. I have had some amazing life experiences that I would otherwise not have had if I had not smiled! A smile has the power to transform or diffuse a situation. A smile saved me more than once from unsavory characters and has given me advantages in my life pursuit of a career and guided me to lifelong friendships.

For example, one night at Lake Tulloc, I met this real gangster looking guy. As I walked by, his friends were harassing a nice defenseless guy for no reason other than being mean spirited and bored. I have always hated bullies so I had a particularly bad reaction to it. I knew I was no physical match for them so I smiled at the smaller gangster guy who was covered from head to toe in tattoos and coming out of the room as I passed bye. I asked him why his friends had to do such a horrible thing. Then I sat on the bench outside his room and cried for humanity. The poor guy was so taken aback that he sat next to me and said "why you got to do that for girl". I explained my issue with the behavior of his friends and soon after we became friends. He said " You are too good. I wish everyone cared about things the way you do. You have no business being out here. Go home. I am going to call you Maria". He then successfully reeled in his friends and offered to walk me home. The next morning we left and drove to the Delta to water Ski. Early that afternoon a boat approached ours sounding like they wanted to pick a fight. I remember thinking "Oh God this is not good" and I was frightened. The three guys I was with looked scared too. There was no doubt this group of men in the other boat wanted a fight. As they approached I tried to muster universal protection energy. As I almost felt myself curling up bracing for impact I heard someone shout "Maria" in a strangely familiar voice. I looked up as he yelled fondly " Maria is that you?" The guys on my boat looked at me and said "who the @&%^#+)* heck is Maria". I looked past them and waved to my new found friend. I then heard him tell the others "they are cool" leave them alone. WHEW! Needless to say I was teasingly called "Maria" all day and milked it for all the free food and drinks I could squeeze from my guy friends under the guise of "protection". HA!

A decade out of college I met my paraplegic friends sister for the first time at a random party and we became friends solely because her brother who was also in attendance told her I was his friend. She was so moved that a complete stranger had made such an impact in her brothers' life that she gave me a second look. I can tell you we were oil and vinegar but that mere act of kindness to her brother bonded two unlikely friends together and formed a whole other wonderful ongoing chapter of my life. Synchronicity at its finest.

In addition, my first real job out of College was given to me by a shy not so popular kid from high school that I befriended with a smile every time I saw him. He remembered me and my acceptance and embracement of him and his brother. I wasn't well qualified for the position of assistant to the Vice President of International Sales at a semi conductor company but it was a great experience. Everyone shook their head at that one! It gave me a solid insight into "it's not what you know but who you know"! HA!

SO a smile is not only fun but it can save your ass, help you to make lifelong friends and maybe even get you a job. Not smiling could and does have the reverse effect! A smile can define you to a degree for the rest of your life. And best of all a smile is free! No matter what happens in life, be good to people . Being good is a wonderful legacy to leave behind. So smile and be kind to everyone you see. Smiles are remembered! You never know who could use a little of your

Star Energy.

Love,

Mom

Jeannine Gallant, 2014

GOSSIP GIRL

"Great minds discuss ideas, average minds discuss events, small minds discuss people"

— Eleanor Roosevelt

Dear Girls,

GOSSIP! Who doesn't love a juicy tidbit about someone else's life? The "no way", "omg", "are you kidding me?!" moments? To have someone's rapt attention as you hold information others want? To hear something intriguing about someone else? Gossip can be downright fun at the moment it's being told. Yet, if you take a step back and really think about it, gossip is truly hurtful. There is no good reason or use for it. I can't think of anyone who likes to be gossiped about. So why, I wonder, is it such a "common" and "normal" practice in our lives? Why do we all accept and contribute to it?

The dictionary defines gossip as "idle talk or rumor, especially about the personal or private affairs of others." The definition alone gives us a picture that gossip is not a positive activity, to talk about someone else's PRIVATE affairs. Yet its still a very common practice both to be the one who gossips, and to enjoy being around someone who does, neither of which, if we were to be truly honest with ourselves, shows a great deal of integrity.

I remember hearing many years ago that gossip hurts at least three people directly: the person engaging in the gossip, the person being told the gossip, and the person the gossip is about. Even though I engage in it both as a person who gossips and a person who listens, I rarely feel good about "gossip sessions". There is a piece of me that always feels dirty, and all too often I wish I could have handled myself differently. What would it have looked like for me to hold my tongue, or to say to a friend, this doesn't feel good, lets not talk about so and so like this?

We gossip for many reasons. Sometimes we engage in this activity to get understanding from someone else. "So and so did this and it doesn't feel right", and your friend might say, oh I know, she did that to me too. Already you feel better because you don't feel crazy, or alone. And sometimes we gossip from an angry, venting place. "So and so did this and I'm so furious I don't know what to do about it, I hope you are as outraged as I am about this and stand by my side in all this anger".

How we gossip is through the filter with which WE see a specific event. Its rarely the whole truth and therefore not portrayed in a fair light. We change the perspective for both ourselves and those around us by telling a story from an emotional space, and we alter someone else's perspective by having them listen.

To say, "I'm never going to be part of gossip again" is not realistic. We all will fall into both contributing and being an active participant. But what would it look like if we just made ourselves more aware of the practice. If every time we thought to gossip, or were part of a gossip session, we just thought, "is this a fair portrayal?" "If this was about me, what would I feel like to hear it?"

Could those two questions alone change the way in which we gossip?

Love,

Auntie Stephanie, December 2014

SAFE HARBOR

"Ships are safe in the harbor but that is not what ships are built for."

— John A. Shedd

My girl,

You were safe the first day you entered into this world. People surrounded us, guided us, nurtured us, allowing you to breathe in that first breath of air. Your safety was all of our concern. From that moment we stood between you and the world. We guarded you in seats, barred you in beds, shielded the sun from your skin and held your hand along the roads. And on the road we took you.

You journeyed across the country to another safe haven of relatives who welcomed you to their side of the world. Along the way we camped, slept, stopped, took photos, met horses, warmed bottles and felt no concern for traveling with our nine-month old daughter.

Within a year, we had journeyed back across the country to a new home in the mountains. It was a safely nestled town with fresh air and views far along the Sierra mountain range. Your first friends were found at the library, where we sang, borrowed books for your little world and became one with our town and the idea of a home..

Traveling did not stop. We journeyed many times back to New York, Florida and areas of California. Adventure called us in the form of an Alaskan home. We buckled you up again, set our sights north and lived in a natural place. We flew across the puddles of water of the tundra, and saw bears, caribou, eagles and plenty of fish. We learned to appreciate pizza in the nearby town 30 miles away as our remote location became the slow life of people, friends, neighbors and long days filled with light.

As we journeyed back to the mountains of California, we stopped in Seattle for over a year. With a new sibling and more new landscapes to breathe in, our family grew and experienced the sights and sounds of more challenging days. From that point on, the seed had been planted. Your traveling days were a way of life.

You were six years old returning to what is now your hometown. We rooted your education in this place but continued to nurture all of our loves of travel. I shared my favorite quote with you from my fourth-grade teacher, "Ships are safe in the harbor but that is not what ships are built for." Because I held her in my heart for instilling this in my life, I had maintained relations with her all of these years. For your thirteenth birthday you received a package from her that contained a small figurine of a vintage sailing ship. You were safe in the harbor but you also knew that there was safety and strength in knowing the world.

You were fifteen-years-old when you first stepped away from us. Watching you walk through the security checkpoint at the airport, eyes wide open and excited for the next step, I knew you would be safe. I didn't think it would be easy, being away from home for 11 months in a country in which you had no grasp of the language. But finding your way in this world was the greatest gift I could give to you for your sixteenth birthday. You returned to us speaking of challenges, sorrow, misdirection and rejection. Each one of these experiences you conquered on your own. In the same conversation, you spoke of finding your way, dancing, laughing, sleeping, historical places, friends from around the world, speaking in front of hundreds and feeling the excitement of returning to your home, your harbor.

Had you not gone through the rhythms of being in a new place, new life, new existence then, you would not be where you are now. You may be some place safe, but you wouldn't carry the creativity, knowledge and most of all authentic gratitude and appreciation of the adventure of life.

As a grown woman, I hope you will continually return to your original harbor. Your life force will be nurtured by the excitement of the returns but, most excitingly for us, you will bring back your new experiences, projects, ideas, photos, friends, lovers and, most importantly, your grateful heart.

Stay buckled in. May the bars you see only be safety guides you can hold on to while you see the world. Keep shielding your skin from the sun, but allow the light to show you the various colors of the world and nurture your creative soul.

We virtually hold your hand along the road and no longer stand between you and the world, but always stand waiting for your next return.

Safe travels my girl,

Love,

Mom

Ursula Riina, December 21, 2013

In Deepest Gratitude and Honor:

I would like to thank the women who took a leap of faith and went on this creative journey with me. I think we each knew how vital it is at this time to reach beyond our day to day lives and connect with the young feminine energy that will be growing into their own wisdom in the coming years.

As women, we lovingly stand on the shoulders of one another as we grow and learn on this sacred journey. We send many blessing to each you as you journey forward and create your own encyclopedia of wisdom.

In deep love and gratitude,

Alaina

Made in the USA
Middletown, DE
27 March 2019